A Collector's Guide To

Movie Memorabilia
WITH PRICES

Anthony Slide

Other books by Anthony Slide
  Early American Cinema (1970)
  The Griffith Actresses (1973)
  The Idols of Silence (1976)
  The Big V: A History of the Vitagraph Company (1976)
  Early Women Directors (1977)
  Aspects of American Film History prior to 1920 (1978)
  Films on Film History (1979)
  The Kindergarten of the Movies: A History of the Fine Arts Company (1980)
  The Vaudevillians (1981)
  Great Radio Personalities in Historic Photographs (1982)

With Edward Wagenknecht
  The Films of D.W. Griffith (1975)
  Fifty Great American Silent Films: 1912-1920 (1980)

Editor
  Selected Film Criticism: 1896–1911 (1982)
  Selected Film Criticism: 1912–1920 (1982)
  Selected Film Criticism: 1921–1930 (1982)
  Selected Film Criticism: 1931–1940 (1982)
  Selected Film Criticism: 1941–1950 (1982)

Pamphlets
  Lillian Gish (1969)
  Sir Michael Balcon (1969)
  The Films of Will Rogers (1979)

Cover photograph by Perry L. Struse, Jr.

Library of Congress
Catalog Card Number 82-62061
ISBN 0-87069-377-8

10 9 8 7 6 5 4 3 2 1

Published by

Wallace-Homestead Book Co.
1912 Grand Avenue
Des Moines, Iowa 50305

Acknowledgments

Thanks are due to the many dealers who answered my questions and took the trouble to send me information concerning their companies. I would particularly like to thank the following: the staff of the Margaret Herrick Library of the Academy of Motion Picture Arts and Sciences: Mike Hawks and Lloyd Douglas of Eddie Brandt's Saturday Matinee; Ernest D. Burns of Cinemabilia; Sam Rubin of *Classic Images;* Phil Luboviski of Larry Edmunds Bookshop; Paul Silliman, vice-president for marketing and sales of National Screen Service Corporation; Steve Chamberlain; Carol Cullen; Robert B. Cushman; Sam Gill; Marty Kearns; Richard Lampurski; Ed Neal; and Herb Sterne.

Color photographs of the majority of lobby cards and posters illustrated in this book may be purchased either from Larry Edmunds Bookshop or Eddie Brandt's Saturday Matinee.

Contents

Introduction

The motion picture is less than one hundred years old, and yet it has probably spawned more diverse memorabilia than any other industry in the world. Still photographs, costumes, props, publicity materials, posters, and lobby cards are created directly by the film industry as part of its activities.

As an adjunct to the cinema's promotional efforts, manufacturers have been licensed to create products as varied as *E.T.* toys, Mickey Mouse watches, film star playing cards, *Gone with the Wind* jigsaw puzzles, and *Photoplay* editions of popular novels. The creation of *Gone with the Wind* memorabilia and Walt Disney-related products has become an industry in itself. In an effort to bring the cinema a little closer, the public has taken to collecting autographs of film personalities with even more fervor than dealers in rare manuscripts and autograph materials exhibit in searching out letters from Abraham Lincoln and early folios of Shakespeare plays.

In more recent times, the public has been given the opportunity to acquire record sound tracks of films as well as videotapes and 8mm and 16mm copies of their favorite motion pictures. There is little question that every household in America owns some item of movie memorabilia, be it merely a single issue of *Photoplay* or a souvenir program for *Ben-Hur* or *South Pacific*.

Value or collectibility has little to do with age as far as movie memorabilia is concerned. Because of a lack of recognizable star names, material from the second decade of this century is less sought after than glamorous items from the 1930s. A 1914 issue of *Photoplay* with John Bunny on its cover is worth almost half of what a 1934 issue of the same magazine with Joan Crawford on its cover would fetch.

Mary Pickford was one of the most famous film personalities in the world, and yet, because her films remained unseen for so many years, collectors are less interested in original photographs of America's Sweetheart than of Buster Keaton, whose films have a continuing cult following. Anything on Humphrey Bogart, Marilyn Monroe, Judy Garland, Joan Crawford, or Al Jolson is eagerly sought, while fascinating and probably unique items of "forgotten" stars such as Anita Stewart, James Hall, Alice White, and Douglas Dick are passed by.

Aside from D.W. Griffith, Erich von Stroheim, and Alfred Hitchcock, directors garner little interest from collectors of movie memorabilia.

One-of-a-kind film equipment from the 1890s or the early 1900s is valued in the hundreds or thousands of dollars, but because it has such little interest to most collectors, it is extremely difficult for an owner to find a prospective purchaser. No dealers specialize in film equipment, and few will even consider handling it. As far as institutional holdings of such equipment are concerned, the only major collections are in the International Museum of Photography at George Eastman House in Rochester, New York, and at the Smithsonian Institution in Washington, D.C. If these institutions have one example of a particular piece of apparatus, there is little chance of their being interested in acquiring another—even if it is the only other known one of its kind.

Thus, it will be appreciated that what is rare or unique is not always of major value to collectors. At the present time, it seems that there will always be a market for one-sheet posters of such recent films as *Star Wars*, *Raiders of the Lost Ark*, and *E.T.*, despite such posters being issued in the tens of thousands. But the owner of an advertising flyer for a 1915 or 1916 feature film—even though there are probably less than a dozen in existence—will be lucky to find a buyer willing to pay more than $2 for one.

"Star quality" is the dominant factor in the value of a specific piece of film memorabilia, be it a one-of-a-kind item or a mass-produced product. It was in 1910 that the film industry first began publicizing its stars in a major way, and it was shortly thereafter that movie companies began distributing to the public postcard photographs of film personalities. In 1911, *The Motion Picture Story Magazine* (later *Motion Picture Magazine*), the cinema's first "fan" magazine, was introduced, to be followed a year later by *Photoplay*. Prior to that period, all promotion of motion pictures was geared exclusively by the distributors and the producers to the exhibitors through "trade" periodicals such as *The Moving Picture World* and *Variety*.

Once the cinema recognized the value to itself of fans, there was no end to the types of paper materials

distributed. In addition, trinkets, dishes featuring drawings of film celebrities, supposed life stories of the stars, programs, and throwaway advertising flyers were all produced in vast quantities. Despite two world wars and the accompanying paper drives a considerable quantity of this type of memorabilia has survived, although its value is small because of the limited interest in the cinema's early years. With the Twenties and the Thirties, fan magazines proliferated, and the studios developed publicity departments aimed solely at catering to the public's fascination with screen personalities. For the cost of a postage stamp, fans could acquire autographed photographs of their favorite stars, photographs that a less naive public would have realized were signed only by the stars' secretaries.

Currently a new sophistication in the marketing of movie memorabilia has been reached, with producers realizing the vast commercial potential of tie-ins with their films and the licensing of toys, posters, and games. The ancillary marketing rights for such novelties can be worth millions of dollars when films like *Star Wars*,

A lobby card for President Reagan's best known feature, *Bedtime for Bonzo*, which might, under ideal conditions, be worth $150.

Annie, and *E.T.* are involved. Just as the popularity of a new film guarantees an expansion of interest in these by-products, so can a historic moment in world events create new value for movie memorabilia.

With the election of Ronald Reagan as president, the value of posters, lobby cards, and photographic stills from Reagan's 1937-1964 film career soared. In a matter of weeks, a poster for a minor Reagan Western, *Tennessee's Partner* (1955), increased in value 500 percent. The only question is, will that same poster decrease 500 percent in value when Reagan ceases to be president. The representative of one auction house notes that in 1980 a poster for the Ronald Reagan vehicle, *Bedtime for Bonzo* (1951), was sold for $600. That same poster today is worth only $200.

Collectors can be divided into two categories. The first group—to whom this book is chiefly directed—is interested exclusively in original items and concerned with building a collection for personal edification, without any thought as to the uses to which such a collection might be put. The collection exists for an individual's personal enjoyment. For want of a better term, these collectors have become known as "film buffs"—and, unfortunately, many serious collectors have been branded by a phrase that, more and more, has come to have a derogatory undertone.

The second group is comprised of those with a serious or scholarly interest in the motion picture. Members of this group will acquire a photographic still for use with a proposed article or book, and it will be irrelevant to them as to whether the still is an original or a copy. This same group is similarly disinterested as to whether a book it purchases is a rare original or a cheap reprint. It is content, not appearance, that is important. The first type of collector has almost no interest in the latest volume on film aesthetics or criticism and is oblivious to what is happening in the world of avant-garde or experimental cinema. Popular cinema, past and present, is the sole concern of this collector of movie memorabilia. Of course, the existence of these two divergent groups makes for a larger potential market for those involved in the selling of memorabilia.

The most ardent of collectors are those of *Gone with the Wind* and Disney-related items. For the former, there is the G.W.T.W. Collectors Club (5 West Old Liberty Road, Sykesville, Md. 21784), which publishes a newsletter with information on current activities, publications, etc., relating to the 1939 feature. In the newsletter, collectors will find photographs, souvenir programs, the film sound track, reprints of original posters, books, matchbooks, and stationery advertised for sale. Hardcore collectors should also be aware of The Gone with the Wind Museum (152 Nassau Street, N.W., Atlanta, Georgia 30303), which boasts "the world's largest *Gone with the Wind* collection," not to mention Melanie's Restaurant and "the finest in Southern Cooking, no entree over $3."

However, *Gone with the Wind* memorabilia is as nothing compared to the amount of Disneyana produced through the years. Ardent collectors will be familiar with the definitive book on the subject: *Disneyana: Walt Disney Collectibles* by Cecil Munsey (Hawthorn Books, 1974). In addition, collectors should be aware of a professionally produced newsletter, *The Disneyana Collector,* published by Grolier Enterprises, Inc., Sherman Turnpike, Danbury, Ct. 06816. This newsletter even features a column titled "Mickey's Mailbox," in which the industrious mouse answers collectors' questions.

The Walt Disney Studio operates its own archives at 500 South Buena Vista Street, Burbank, California 91521, but these are only open to bona fide researchers and use by "fans" is discouraged. Surplus memorabilia may often be found at the souvenir shop at Disneyland in Anaheim, California, and it is surprising the exceedingly rare items that can be found there—although, unfortunately, the rarity of the item is always matched by the price.

This volume is intended to provide both the beginner and the avid collector with detailed background information on movie memorabilia, offering background on the various types available, the dealers who specialize in such material, and the current market value of these items. The prices quoted here are intended only as a guide and are based on those current at the time of publication. However, as the recent astronomical prices paid at auction for both movie fan and trade items indicate, collecting movie memorabilia can be both an enjoyable hobby and a sound financial investment.

1 Books

There is no accurate count of the number of books concerned with film published since the cinema came into being in the 1890s. The Margaret Herrick Library of the Academy of Motion Picture Arts and Sciences has some fifteen thousand English language volumes in its collection, and there are probably almost the same number published in other languages. One thing is certain, however: film books tend to bring out the worst qualities in both writers and critics, and the only way for a collector to decide what books he or she wants is by reading them.

From a collector's viewpoint, virtually all film books of recent vintage have no value and are unlikely to have any appreciable monetary value in the future. It would be easy to claim that no film books published in the last ten years have increased in value. The majority have, in fact, decreased. Certainly 90 percent of all film books published in 1983 will be on the remainder tables of your local bookshops by 1984 or 1985. The exceptions are books from publishers such as Scarecrow, G.K. Hall, and R.R. Bowker that specialize in literature for the library market and the scholarly community and publish in such small quantities that it would be financially out of the question to remainder their product.

Collectors should also bear in mind that many film books are published in editions of two thousand copies or less, and that after a book has gone through the remainder process all surviving copies still in the hands of the publisher will be "pulped" (destroyed). This can mean that there are possibly fewer than a thousand copies of some fairly recent film books still extant, and the majority of those are probably in libraries and unlikely to reach the collectors' market.

As an example, this writer and Edward Wagenknecht were responsible for a book titled *The Films of D.W. Griffith,* which Crown published for the Griffith Centennial in 1975. The book sold only 1,800 copies before it was remaindered at under $5 (compared to the published price of $12.95). When the book did not sell particularly well at its remainder price, the publisher withdrew all copies from bookshops and had them destroyed. As a consequence, copies of *The Films of D.W. Griffith* are not that easy to find, and now sell at used bookstores at prices averaging $15.

Jack Mathis' stupendous volume on Republic serials, *Valley of the Cliffhangers,* was published in 1975 at $50. Long out of print, it is now valued at double that amount. Similarly, *Four Fabulous Faces* by Larry Carr, which offered beautifully reproduced photographs of Greta Garbo, Gloria Swanson, Joan Crawford, and Marlene Dietrich in a single volume selling at its publication in 1970 at $40, now brings (in that first original printing only) $100 or more. It remains to be seen if Ronald Haver's sumptuous volume on *David O. Selznick's Hollywood,* first published in 1980 at $85, will rise in value or whether the large quantity of copies that the publisher must have produced to make the project a viable one will keep the book available to collectors at less than its published price.

In considering the future value of current film books, the basic rule would seem to be: Does the book have a unique aspect, such as excellent reproduction of photographs, or a particularly controversial topic? Also bear in mind that a book published by a small, obscure firm such as Paul Spehr's *The Movies Begin* (published in 1977 by the Newark Museum) is and will continue to be harder to find than a book from a major New York publishing house such as Simon and Schuster or Harper and Row.

General film books, be they biographies, autobiographies or histories, published from the Thirties through the Fifties can usually be acquired for an average price of $10 to $15. This applies to anything from film pioneer Albert E. Smith's autobiography, *Two Reels and a Crank* (1952), to Paul Rotha's pioneering work of film scholarship, *The Film Till Now* (1930). *Upton Sinclair Presents William Fox* (1933), Robert C. Cannom's study of veteran director W.S. "Woody" Van Dyke, *Van Dyke and the Mythical City, Hollywood* (1948), and Will Irwin's authorized biography of Paramount Pictures co-founder Adolph Zukor, *The House That Shadows Built* (1928), are all approximately equal in monetary and research value and collectors' interest.

However, in fixing an average bookstore price, collectors are reminded that what a prominent specialist book-

seller charges can be comparatively high when compared to prices at a run-of-the-mill bookshop or at a typical used book sale at a local public library, where film books often sell for as low as thirty-five cents per copy.

There are exceptions, of course, and one such group consists of the occasional volumes of film scripts published in anthologies. The first such anthology was Frances Taylor Patterson's *Motion Picture Continuities* (1929), which featured screenplays for three silent features: *A Kiss for Cinderella, The Scarlet Letter,* and *The Last Command.* Fairly scarce today, this volume can sell for as high as $35. At around $25, one may find copies of a group of script anthologies published in the late Thirties and early Forties: *Four Star Scripts,* edited by Lorraine Noble (1936) and including *Lady for a Day, It Happened One Night, Little Women,* and *The Story of Louis Pasteur; The Best Pictures, 1939-1940,* edited by Jerry Wald and Richard Macaulay (1940); *Twenty Best Film Plays,* edited by John Gassner and Dudley Nichols (1943); *The Best Film Plays of 1943-1944,* edited by

The cluttered interior of Larry Edmunds Bookshop, Hollywood.

Gassner and Nichols (1945), and *The Best Film Plays of 1945*, edited by Gassner and Nichols (1946).

A British publisher produced one of the first scripts for a sound feature, *Jew Süss* (1935), but because the film is fairly obscure this volume is worth only $10. Film scripts have continued to be published to the present. The Viking Press was at one time active with a series titled "The MGM Library of Film Scripts," which included single volume screenplays for *Ninotchka*, *North by Northwest*, *Adam's Rib*, and *A Day at the Races*, among others. Currently the University of Wisconsin Press is publishing, in both paperback and hard cover editions, the Warner Bros. screenplay series.

For those interested in acquiring actual mimeographed scripts rather than published and edited versions, there are a number of problems. First, the film studios maintain that their scripts were never given away to technicians or performers and always remained the property of the studio. It could, therefore, be legally argued that all unpublished screenplays remain the property of the film company that produced the film regardless of where a collector might have acquired his copy of the script. Some producers have made threatening noises toward bookshops openly selling copies of film and television scripts, but as yet no legal decision appears to have been made regarding the validity of such sales. An original screenplay for a classic film such as *Citizen Kane* (1941) or *The Wizard of Oz* (1939) can sell for as much as $250, while screenplays for fairly recent and minor features may sometimes be found at thrift shops or similar outlets in Los Angeles selling for as little as $5.

Strangely, the type of screenplay does not appear to affect the price. Thus, an early draft of a script can be worth as much to a collector as the final shooting script (used for the actual production of a film) or a cutting continuity (a script exact in every detail to the finished feature used for editing purposes). The only exception is a script used by a director or a leading performer in a film. It will often be annotated and may even be autographed by the entire cast and crew, but such screenplays seldom come on the market and when they do sell for $200 or more.

In addition to screenplays, a considerable number of books on the making of individual films continues to be published. Among the more interesting from the past are Michael Powell's *200,000 Feet: The Edge of the World* (1939), and *Grass* by Merian C. Cooper (1925), about the making of the Paramount-released documentary, which includes sixty-four photographs by Cooper's partner, Ernest Schoedsack. Two volumes that have literary as well as film interest are *The Forgotten Village* by John Steinbeck (1941), which includes one hundred thirty-six photographs from the film, and Jean Cocteau's *Diary of a Film* (1950), which chronicles the making of the French classic, *La Belle et la Bête*.

Books from the silent era—those published prior to 1928—have considerably more value, but here again there are exceptions. From about 1916 through the Twenties a sizable number of books on writing for the screen were published. Today everyone wants to be a director, but it seems that back then everyone wanted to be a screenwriter, and publishers and minor writers were happy to oblige the public whim by turning out dozens of volumes on the subject.

All of these books have little monetary value and even less literary worth. One company, the Palmer Photoplay Corporation, also known as the Palmer Institute of Authorship, the brainchild of one Frederick Palmer, produced a whole series of books, including *Photoplay Plots and Plot Sources* (1920) and *Technique of the Photoplay* (1924). Additionally, Palmer published a series of books dealing with various aspects of film production. Valued at $5 each, these unique little documents include Al Christie's *The Elements of Situation Comedy*, Clarence Badger's *The Point of Attack, or How To Start the Photoplay*, George Beban's *Photoplay Characterization*, and Jeanie MacPherson's *The Necessity and Value of Theme in the Photoplay*.

Many fascinating and colorful pamphlets appeared during the silent years. The Little Movie Mirror Books contained photographs and essays on the likes of Viola Dana, William S. Hart, Bert Lytell, Wallace Reid, and Ben Turpin. Published in the early Twenties at 10 cents each, these small booklets now sell for $12 apiece. There is no accurate record of the quantity or types of such booklets published. They include everything from Larry Trimble on *The Story of Strongheart* (a rival to Rin-Tin-Tin), published in 1924, to Sally O'Neil's 1929 pamphlet, *Follywood—and How!*, "the only complete and authentic story of the discovery and rise of the wonder girl of the movie as written by herself for her fans thruout the world."

The best known of books published in the Twenties and a classic of the cinema is Terry Ramsaye's *A Million and One Nights* (1926). The first major history of the cinema, it appeared initially as a series of articles in *Photoplay*. The first, limited edition of *A Million and One Nights* was signed by Thomas Edison and is valued at $250 or more, while the popular editions published at the same time—a deluxe edition in blue almost the size of the limited edition and a smaller red-bound edition—can be found for around $150 per two-volume set. A few years ago, a first edition of *A Million and One Nights* signed by a group of pioneers of the cinema—including Mary Pickford and Adolph Zukor—was sold by a New York book dealer for $750. *A Million and One Nights* has been reprinted in a hard cover library edition and in a popular, one-volume, paperback edition by Simon and Schuster (1964).

Other rare volumes from the silent era, for which $50 is an average price, include *Let's Go to the Movies* by Iris Barry (1926); *Motion Picture Work* by David S. Hulfish (1915); *Behind the Motion Picture Screen* by Austin C. Lescarboura (1919); *Moving Pictures: How They Are Made and Worked* by Frederick A. Talbot (1914); and *The Art of the Moving Picture* by Vachel Lindsay (1915 and 1922). Despite its off-putting title, *Motion Picture Acting* by Frances Agnew (1913) contains some useful essays by early film performers such as John Bunny and is well worth $15. *The Best Moving Pictures of 1922-23*, edited by noted critic Robert E. Sherwood, is well worth $50 with its lengthy essays on sixteen feature films, its short commentaries on thirty-five more, its listing of all films released in the United States between June, 1922, and June, 1923, and its biographical section on more than four hundred film personalities.

Robert Grau's 1914 volume, *The Theatre of Science*, was subtitled "A volume of progress and achievement in the motion picture art." It provides a solid, firsthand account of the growth of the film industry and was initially published in a limited edition of three thousand copies. Today it is valued at $75 or more. *The Theatre of Science* and many of the other volumes mentioned here have been reprinted in recent years by Arno Press, Benjamin Blom, and others, but, obviously, serious collectors are interested only in original editions. Many of the reprints are now priced almost as high as the first printings.

Douglas Fairbanks, Sr. authored two early volumes concerning his philosophy of life, *Laugh and Live* (1917) and *Making Life Worthwhile* (1918), but because the books are dull and Fairbanks has little cult appeal, each volume can easily be acquired for between $5 and $10. The same is not true of serial queen Pearl White's highly fictitious autobiography, *Just Me* (1919), which is scarce and sells for $50 or more. A similar price can be placed on Charlie Chaplin's 1922 record of his visit to Europe, *My Trip Abroad*. A price of $25 is a good one for a first edition of Harold Lloyd's autobiography, *An American Comedy* (1928), co-authored with Wesley W. Stout, and for Mrs. D.W. Griffith's fascinating account of the early years of filmmaking at the Biograph Company, *When the Movies Were Young* (1925). One of the first producers to write his autobiography was Samuel Goldwyn with *Behind the Screen* (1923), and it is another good buy at $25.

Another early autobiography, William S. Hart's *My Life East and West* (1928), is reasonably priced at $20 and would be worth more except that Hart has never held much interest for collectors, even for those specializing in the Western. It is curious that Western enthusiasts display such little excitement over Hart, Tom Mix, Hoot Gibson, Harry Carey, and other great cowboy heroes from the silent era, preferring to save their adulation for the likes of Gene Autry, Roy Rogers, Jock Mahoney,

Sunset Carson, Yakima Canutt, and others from the Thirties and Forties, who can be seen at conventions wandering around like specters from the past, sporting oversize cowboy hats and pot bellies.

One of the first volumes devoted to the personalities of the cinema was *Who's Who in the Film World*, an extremely scarce volume valued at $100 or more. One of the best of the early biographical studies is Carolyn Lowrey's *The First One Hundred Noted Men and Women of the Screen* (1920), which features fairly accurate and detailed essays, plus one hundred full-page photographs, and is a good buy at $50. (Occasionally leather-bound editions of this book can be found, often with the gold-embossed name of one of the individuals featured in the volume on the cover.) Other rare versions of who's who include *Famous Film Folk* by Charles Donald Fox (1925), and *Famous Stars of Filmdom: Women* (1931) and *Famous Stars of Filmdom: Men* (1932), both by Elinor Hughes.

For researchers and collectors alike, the *Motion Picture News Studio Directory*, first published in 1916 and appearing regularly through the mid-Twenties, is a valuable source of information, becoming increasingly rare these days and selling for $75 and more an issue. (The first volume was paperbound, but all the others have cloth covers.) In 1929 and 1930, the same periodical published *Motion Picture News Blue Book*, "the authoritative who's who of filmdom," now selling for between $30 and $50. For $50, it is possible to acquire either *The Picturegoer's Who's Who and Encyclopedia of the Screen Today* or Clarence Winchester's *The World Film Encyclopedia*, both published in Great Britain in 1933, and containing much more information than mere biographical entries. *Winchester's Screen Encyclopedia*, published in 1948—again in Great Britain—and edited by Maud M. Miller, is a reasonable purchase at $75, containing as it does entries on more than one thousand film personalities, as well as essays by everyone from composer Muir Mathieson to producer Alexander Korda and pioneer Cecil Hepworth to producer Adolph Zukor. Another Clarence Winchester publication, little known in this country, is *The Wonder Album of Filmland* (1933), with one hundred ninety-two pages of photographs of stars of the day, and currently selling for $55.

Photoplay magazine published at least three volumes of photographs of film personalities with capsule biographies of each in 1916, 1924, and 1930. Each book is valued at $50. Casting directories, containing photographs of performers and information about the agents who represent them, are becoming increasingly popular with collectors. *The Standard Casting Directory*, which began publication in the mid-Twenties, sells for around $20 a copy, while *The Cast*, a quarterly directory from the early Thirties with expensive binding and exquisitely reproduced photographs, can be worth $25 or more. The British casting directory *Spotlight*, which began publication in the Thirties, is seldom found in early editions in the United States and yet is fairly reasonably priced at $10 or $15. The best known of all casting directories is the *Academy Players Directory*, currently published three times a year in a four-volume edition for $55. The *Academy Players Directory* was first published in 1937 as *Academy Players Bulletin*, and that first edition was recently reprinted by the Academy of Motion Picture Arts and Sciences (8949 Wilshire Boulevard, Beverly Hills, Calif. 90211) in a soft cover version for $12 and in hard cover for $25.

There are, of course, books relating to the motion picture published earlier than this century. Thomas Edison's assistant, W.K.L. Dickson, who probably had far more to do with the invention of the motion picture than his employer, co-authored what is generally considered to be the first volume to discuss the cinema, *History of the Kinetograph, Kinetoscope and Kinetophonograph*, published in 1895. Although privately printed in the Thirties (by cinematographer Charles G. Clarke and a collectors' item in this edition) and more recently by Arno Press, an original of the Dickson volume is worth $200 or more. Also from the 1890s, Henry V. Hopwood's *Living Pictures* (1899) and C. Francis Jenkins' *Animated Pictures* (1898) are equally rare and will sell for $100 or more.

Magic lanterns, optical toys, and other items associated with the period prior to the invention of the motion picture per se are classified as pre-cinema. The first book to discuss the magic lantern and the first volume with any relevance to the motion picture is Athanasius Kircher's *Ars Magna Lucis et Umbrae*, published initially in 1646 and reprinted in a revised edition in 1671. Naturally, copies of these books would be worth many thousands of dollars. Somewhat less valuable are the publications dealing with the magic lantern from the nineteenth century, such as W.J. Chadwick's *The Magic Lantern Manual* (1878), A.E. Dolbear's *The Art of Projecting* (1877), and T.C. Hepworth's *The Book of the Lantern* (1894).

Curiously, a fairly recent book on pre-cinema, Olive Cook's *Movement in Two Dimensions* (1963), described as "a study of the animated and projected pictures which preceded the invention of cinematography," appears to have been distributed in an extremely limited edition, and is something of a collector's item, selling for $20 or more.

Almost equal in value to the Athanasius Kircher volume is a collection of the original eleven volumes of Eadweard Muybridge's *Animal Locomotion*, consisting of seven hundred eighty-one plates and published by the University of Pennsylvania in 1887. Muybridge, an

Cinemabilia, New York.

Englishman working in the United States, was noted for the series of photographs of moving objects with which he experimented under the sponsorship of Leland Stanford in the early 1870s, and for the invention of the zoopraxiscope, which projected such animated photographs upon a screen. This was a forerunner to the cinema a few years later. Muybridge's photographs also have a less scientific interest—the majority of them are of naked men, women, and children, and to judge by the smirks on some of the subjects' faces, the involvement of the models was not entirely academic. For the serious scholar, the original 1887 edition of *Animal Locomotion* was reprinted by Dover Publications in 1979 at the more reasonable price of $80. Prior to *Animal Locomotion*, Muybridge had published *The Horse in Motion* in an edition of three thousand copies, and despite such a small printing the book remains available and affordable at between $300 and $500.

Photoplay Editions—popular printings of novels recently filmed, with scene stills inserted in the text—have always been highly collectible. *Photoplay Editions* were first published in 1913, and they continued to be produced in quantity—usually by Grosset and Dunlap—through the Thirties. The average price for a *Photoplay Edition* is $5, although it may be considerably higher when a major film or star is involved, and if the dust jacket which seems so often to be missing, is present.

The only reference work on these types of books is *Photoplay Edition* by Emil Petaja (published in 1975 by Sisu of San Francisco). Petaja notes that the last major *Photoplay Edition* to be published by Grosset and Dunlap was for *Gone with the Wind* (1939), although a form of *Photoplay Editions* continues to be published by other companies on an occasional basis. The average number of illustrations in a *Photoplay Edition* can vary from four to sixteen, and collectors should be aware that there can sometimes be up to three different versions of a *Photoplay Edition* on an individual film, with each version having a different colored cover and even different illustrations.

Similar to the American *Photoplay Editions* was the British series, *Readers Library*, published on an extremely cheap type of paper and originally sold by F.W. Woolworth for sixpence (a nickel) a copy. *Readers Library* editions are fairly rare in the United States, but because of the paper and the binding are not recommended for collection. In the Forties, a British publisher, World Film Publications, produced a series of eighty-page paperback fictionalizations of such films as *The Way to the Stars* (1945) and *Spring in Park Lane* (1948). Mention should also be made of the *Big Little Books* of the Thirties, published by Whitman of Racine, Wisconsin. These volumes are of more interest to collectors of comic books than of movie memorabilia, but a number of volumes are devoted to film subjects.

Finally, collectors should be aware of filmed novels that contain no reference to the movies within the books themselves, but do have dust jackets featuring colorful likenesses of the stars of the productions. A typical novel was the one for *The Gorgeous Hussy* (1936), with a beautiful color drawing of Joan Crawford in the film version on the jacket. A volume such as this with its dust jacket can fetch $10 and yet be worth only a few cents without that precious covering.

Hollywood is more a state of mind than a place, and today it is a dirty mind and a tarnished spot, but there have been a few books on the city of Hollywood. *Hollywood: The First Hundred Years* by Bruce Torrence (1979) is an excellent photographic survey. Edwin O. Palmer's *History of Hollywood*, published in two volumes in 1937, is the best of an earlier age and a bargain at $100. For $125, one can purchase J. Detweiler's *Who's Who in California* (1929), "being a history of California as illustrated in the lives of the builders and defenders of the state and of the men and women who are doing the work and molding the thought of the present time," and containing a good number of film personalities. *Los Angeles Times* writer Harry Carr was responsible for *Los Angeles: City of Dreams* (1935), a highly personalized view of the city, and a bargain at $10.

Annuals and yearbooks have long proven to be popular collectors' items. First published in 1918 as *Wid's Film Daily Yearbook*, *The Film Daily Yearbook* was a standard Hollywood reference work until it ceased publication in 1970. Although available in reprint form, original editions of the *Yearbook* from 1917–19 and the early Twenties are just about impossible to locate. Later editions from the Twenties sell for $75 each, from the Thirties for $40, and from the Forties for $30. Later volumes will sell for between $25 and $10. *The Motion Picture Almanac* began publication in its present format in 1933, and editions from that decade sell for an average of $40. A Forties' edition of *Motion Picture Almanac* sells for approximately $25, one from the Fifties for $20, and one from the Sixties for $10. Editions of *Motion Picture Almanac* that are scarce are those published in a larger format between 1929 and 1932, and, if located, can expect to sell for $50 or more. Because of the industry concentration on the West Coast, copies of *The Film Daily Yearbook* and *The Motion Picture Almanac* tend to sell for much less and be much more available in Los Angeles than in New York.

Film Daily Yearbook and *Motion Picture Almanac* are the standard reference books for the American film industry. Their British rivals were *The Bioscope Annual and Trade Dictionary*, first published in 1910, and *The Kinematograph Yearbook*, first published in 1914. Almost impossible to find in this country, early editions of these yearbooks sell for $150 or more in Great Britain. In 1930 and 1931, the American Society of Cinema-

A 1921 *Little Movie Mirror Book* featuring Viola Dana, value $12.

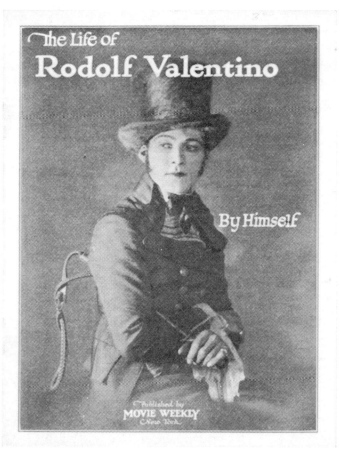

The Life of Rudolph Valentino, published in the early Twenties by *Movie Weekly,* value $15.

tographers published a *Cinematographic Annual,* with each volume containing a wealth of valuable technical and historical information. The 1930 volume is fairly common at $25 or less, but Volume II is extremely hard to find and despite having a smaller number of pages can sell for more than double the price of the 1930 edition.

The British were the first to start publishing film annuals for a general audience with *The Picture Show Annual* (from the Twenties onwards), *The Filmgoers' Annual* (from the Thirties), *The Film-Lovers' Annual* (from the Thirties), *Film Pictorial Annual* (from the Thirties), *The Picturegoer Annual* (from the Thirties onwards), *Ivy Crane Wilson's Hollywood Album* (from the Forties onwards), and *Preview Annual* (from the Fifties). With their colored photographs and their first-hand accounts of the film industry by the stars (all, of course, ghost-written by publicists), these annuals have proven particularly popular with collectors and sell for between $15 and $50 each.

F. Maurice Speed's *Film Review,* first published in 1944 and still going strong, is one of the few annuals with any reference value and a bargain at $15 an edition. Speed remembers how the annual came into being: "I had mentioned the idea during the war to Sheila Van

Damm, who thought it a damn good idea (sorry) and introduced me to Robbie Lantz. Robbie was enthusiastic and sent me off to Hutchinson, who wanted me to sign up to produce the book at the end of paper rationing. Robbie advised against this, and sent me off to Macdonalds, who through connections with the printer Purnell had plenty of spare paper. They produced about 60,000 the first year as I recall, a figure that reached 250,000 (incredible as it may sound at this point of time, but don't forget the public was starved of books because of the paper situation) by the second or maybe third volume. The resultant royalties, by the way, bought me my first house, first new car . . . and my first wife."

Speed also authored a number of Forties pamphlets, including *Movie Cavalcade,* "the story of the cinema, its stars, studios and producers," published annually between 1942 and 1946; *Film Favorites,* and *Stars of the Screen.* Each is worth only $5.

The American version of Speed's *Film Review* is Daniel Blum's *Screen World,* first published in 1949 and edited since 1966 by John Willis. (There was no volume of *Screen World* published in 1950.) A complete run of *Screen World* from 1948–1981 was recently sold by a New York bookseller for $1,400.

15

There are two major sources for new and old film books, one on the East Coast and one on the West. In Los Angeles, Larry Edmunds Bookshop (6658 Hollywood Boulevard, Hollywood, Calif. 90028/213-463-3273), operated by the Luboviski family, is the largest bookshop of its kind in the world. In its cramped quarters, one may find every conceivable film book, as well as stills, posters, lobby cards, and an equally extraordinary collection of theatre volumes. Larry Edmunds Bookshop operates a mail order service, and many libraries place a standing order here to receive automatically one copy of every new film book as it is published. (In case any collectors might be interested in placing such a standing order and as an indication of the amount of film books that continue to be published, the cost would amount to $6,000 or $7,000 annually.)

In New York, Cinemabilia (10 West Thirteenth Street, New York, N.Y. 10011/212-989-8519) is the first stop for collectors. Ernest Burns' store has a smaller stock than Larry Edmunds, but his quarters are considerably less cluttered. In the past, both Larry Edmunds and Cinemabilia have published excellent catalogs of memorabilia. Two bookshops that offer a general variety of used books but feature major sections on film books are the Strand Book Store (828 Broadway, New York, N.Y. 10003/212-473-1452) and Book City (6625 Hollywood Boulevard, Hollywood, Calif. 90028/213-466-0120). Book City is more expensive than Strand, but has a far wider selection of books. The turnover at Book City appears to be small, but to find a bargain at Strand it is almost necessary to pay daily visits to the bookshop.

J-N Herlin (68 Thompson Street, New York, N.Y. 10012/212-431-8732) always has some interesting items in his catalogs and is now able to welcome walk-in customers at his new location. Richard Stoddard (90 East Tenth Street, New York, N.Y. 10003/212-982-9440) specializes chiefly in theatre books, but always has a good selection of rare film books in stock at basically reasonable prices. Theatricana, Inc. (Box 4244, Campus Station, Athens, Ga. 30602/404-548-2514) is another theatrical bookseller, as its title suggests, but each issue of the company's mail order catalog will include a number of unusual film books and periodicals. The best of the mail order outlets is Hampton Books (Route 1, Box 202, Newberry, S.C. 29108/803-276-6870), whose voluminous catalogs are collectors' items in their own right. Hampton Books also publishes *CTVD*, an unusual periodical providing summaries of film and television articles from foreign language magazines.

Other film bookshops include Gotham Book Mart (41 West Forty-seventh Street, New York, N.Y. 10036); Drama Bookshop (723 Seventh Avenue, New York, N.Y. 10019); Theatre Books (1576 Broadway, New York, N.Y. 10036); Drama Books (511 Geary Street, San Francisco,

The cover from the Grosset and Dunlap Photoplay Edition of *The Divine Lady*, a 1929 Corinne Griffith feature.

Calif. 94102); Limelight Bookstore (1803 Market Street, San Francisco, Calif. 94103); Burbank Book Castle (200 North Golden Mall, Burbank, Calif. 91502); and Aladdin Books and Memorabilia (122 West Commonwealth Avenue, Fullerton, Calif. 92631). In Britain, the Cinema Bookshop (13–14 Great Russell Street, London W.C.1) long ago became established as that country's answer to Larry Edmunds. For mail order in England, A.E. Cox (21 Cecil Road, Itchen, Southampton, S02 7HX) and Movies (36 Meon Road, London W3 8AN) are highly recommended.

Elsewhere in the world, film book collectors will feel at home at Arnold Busck (Fiolstraede 24, Copenhagen, Denmark); Librairie Contacts (24 Rue du Colisée, 75008 Paris, France); Le Minotaure (2 rue des Beaux Arts, 75006 Paris, France); Le Zinzin d'Hollywood (7 rue des Ursulines, 75005 Paris, France); Filmland Presse (Aventistrasse 4–6, D-8 Munich 40, West Germany); H. Lindemanns Buchhandlung (Nadlerstrasse 4, D-7000 Stuttgart 1, West Germany); and Filmbuchhandlung Hans Rohr (Oberdorfstrasse 3, 8024 Zurich, Switzerland).

A collection of rare books and periodicals from the Margaret Herrick Library of the Academy of Motion Picture Arts and Sciences.

2 Autographs

One factor that can increase the value of any book, considerably, is whether it is autographed, not by the author (whose signature is probably valueless), but by a personality or a group of personalities associated with the volume. For example, a copy of Iris Barry's 1940 Museum of Modern Art monograph *D.W. Griffith: American Film Master* is worth $15 in good condition, but if signed by its subject (who died in 1948), it is worth $500. Raymond Klune, the production manager on *Gone with the Wind*, recently donated to the library of the Academy of Motion Picture Arts and Sciences a copy of Margaret Mitchell's novel. It was autographed by the film's stars—Clark Gable, Vivien Leigh, Leslie Howard, and Olivia de Havilland—director Victor Fleming, producer David O. Selznick, and nineteen other members of the cast. A prominent Los Angeles autograph dealer evaluated that volume at $2,500.

However, one should not always assume that an autograph increases a book's value. Some celebrities are too enthusiastic about putting their names to paper, and it is rarer to find a copy of Sophie Tucker's autobiography, *Some of These Days* (1945), unsigned than signed. Tucker's place as America's number one autograph giver has been assumed by Jane Withers, whose signature glorifies still photographs, books, lobby cards, programs, posters—in fact, anything with which the former child star was associated. (Happily, as Jane Withers is always anxious to purchase anything associated with her career, the value of such items remains fairly high.)

Autograph hunting was once an innocent occupation, chiefly for young people, that involved hanging around outside a studio, a theatre, a restaurant, or a nightspot in the hope of obtaining the autograph of a prominent, or perhaps not so prominent, personality. Today, unfortunately, autographs have become big business, and many collectors behave in an unethical fashion. Former stars trying to live in quiet seclusion are daily inundated with dozens of items of mail from so-called fans, demanding autographs. These "fans" do not simply request one autograph, but instruct the star to sign six or more index cards.

Many fans lie about their interest in a particular performer, pretending to have seen a film which sometimes does not even exist anymore. It has become a sickening hobby, and most former celebrities have been turned off to autograph collectors. They are fully aware that the writer is planning to sell those signed index cards, and, as a result, many personalities have made arrangements with their post offices to return all suspicious items of mail as undeliverable.

Silent stars such as Laura La Plante, May McAvoy, Mary Brian, and Lois Wilson tell me that to answer requests for autographs would require their spending half of each day doing nothing else. And they do not need their fans anymore. They are happily retired and might well ask where those fans were when they were needed—at the time the studios were ending the careers of many of the big personalities of the silent era. When they receive requests for autographed photographs, such stars wonder where the writer imagines they are to find them or why they would wish to spend money having new photographs made.

There are some major stars of the past, notably Lillian Gish, who are still happy to hear from fans, and willing—and financially able—to answer requests for autographs. As to the value of autographs from living personalities, suffice it to say that a signed card by most is worth little

Autographed 1978 Christmas card from Mary Pickford and Buddy Rogers, value $12.

A copy of Margaret Mitchell's novel, *Gone with the Wind*, signed by the entire cast, value $2,500.

Autographed photograph of Theda Bara, inscribed to her sister, value $150.

more than $5, while an autographed photograph may be valued at $10 or $15. Exceptions are those by some current stars who are disinterested in answering requests for autographs either by mail or in person. Among this group are Jane Fonda, Barbra Streisand, Marlon Brando, and Alan Alda. (Alda, reputedly, has always refused to sign, and his signature may eventually become as rare as that of Garbo.)

How do autograph hunters contact their victims? Some write to a personality through an agency, a business manager, or a studio, but generally such letters are either destroyed or returned to their senders. The major source

for home addresses of the stars (past and present) is *The Ultimate Movie, TV and Rock Directory,* compiled by Roger and Karen Christensen (and published by the Cardiff-by-the-Sea Publishing Company, P.O. Box 909, Cardiff-by-the-Sea, Calif. 92007). The 366 pages of this unique book contain not only addresses for thousands of personalities, but also lists of memorabilia dealers, fan clubs, publications, and a rich assortment of facsimile autographs.

As already noted, the signatures of most living film personalities have only nominal value. One extraordinary exception is Greta Garbo, who never signs for fans today and never signed in the past. Her signature occasionally turns up for sale, usually in connection with a legal document, seldom if ever on a photograph, and is valued at $1,500 or more. A Garbo signature is as valuable as Abraham Lincoln's and worth ten times that of Franklin D. Roosevelt. Ronald Reagan's signature, under certain circumstances, can be even more valuable. In 1981 a hand-written letter from the president was sold for $12,500, but that value had as much to do with the content of the letter as the signature.

Many autograph collectors prefer to specialize in a particular genre. The collecting of signatures of Academy Award winners has always proven popular, as has the collecting of first-day covers signed by those associated with a particular commemorative stamp—and when the stamp celebrates the fiftieth anniversary of talking pictures there is plenty of scope. Autograph dealers recommend collecting signatures or signed photographs of Ginger Rogers and Fred Astaire together, Fay Wray in *King Kong*, or a group of horror film stars such as Christopher Lee, Vincent Price, and Peter Cushing. Most dealers maintain that signatures of these and others will quadruple or more in value in the next ten years. Between 1975 and 1980, Viola Dana's signature on a photograph increased in value from $5 to $15.

In an interview with *The Saturday Evening Post*, noted autograph dealer Charles Hamilton commented, "I predict that autographs of such stars as Elizabeth Taylor, Paul Newman, Henry Fonda, and James Cagney will be very, very valuable in the years to come." With Fonda's death that prediction has already become partially true, and it could well be that the remaining stars who are still fairly agreeable to signing autographs may decide to call a halt and thereby automatically increase the worth of their signatures.

The values placed on film-related autographs range from $1,500 or more for a Lon Chaney, Sr. signature to $15 for that of Mary Astor. Valentino's signature can be worth $500, while Humphrey Bogart, Bela Lugosi, and Clark Gable autographs are valued at around $200 each. Value is determined by several factors such as if the signature is on a card or a photograph; if in ink or pencil; if it was signed at the height of a personality's career or after retirement; if it is on a letter, then the importance of the content of that letter; and if the item is merely signed or both inscribed and signed.

Obviously, the crucial question in collecting autographs is whether a particular signature is genuine. In the past, stars seldom if ever signed photographs requested by fans, but rather had secretaries at the studios where they were under contract take care of such requests. Apparently Jean Harlow had her mother handle this chore for her. Joan Crawford, an avid letter writer who acknowledged every request from a fan up to her

An inscribed photograph of Roscoe "Fatty" Arbuckle, dating from the late Twenties, and worth $200.

death, signed most of her own correspondence, but also had a secretary who would sometimes sign on her behalf. In the last few years of her life, Mary Pickford was physically incapable of signing letters or photographs and had her husband, Buddy Rogers, or a secretary sign for her. In Pickford's case, it is just about impossible to tell which is her signature and which is not.

In more recent years, many major personalities from all walks of life, notably presidents and political figures, have used machines—sometimes called autopens or Signa-Signers—into which a signature and sample of handwriting can be programmed. This machine can be used to sign photographs or even write personal letters, and the handwriting is almost indistinguishable from the real thing—except that the writing is almost too perfect when compared to a genuine signature. An enthusiastic autograph collector and dealer named Tom Parry, who was also editor and publisher of *Newsreel* magazine, revealed that John Wayne utilized a Signa-Signer machine to sign all fans' requests from 1978 onwards. Parry also compiled an incomplete listing of those contemporary personalities who utilize others to sign letters, photographs, and memorabilia, and it includes Elizabeth Taylor, Richard Burton, Richard Dreyfuss, Bob Hope, Charles Bronson, Robert Wagner, Mary Tyler Moore, Jackie Coogan, Angie Dickinson, Howard Duff,

An inscribed photograph of a somber Harry Langdon, dating from the late Twenties, and worth $100.

A rare photograph signed by all four Marx Brothers, value $200.

Billie Dove, Liza Minnelli, Greer Garson, Sylvester Stallone, Fred MacMurray, Bonita Granville, Raquel Welsh, Erik Estrada, and Leonard Nimoy.

Newsreel, which began publication in a mimeographed format in June of 1978, is now published by Bob Bennett at One Governor's Lane, Shelburne, Vt. 05482. It remains the most valuable source of information on collecting film-related autographs, featuring articles on movie personalities, autograph dealers and collectors, plus the latest news from the field, lists of addresses, and advertising from both prominent and lesser-known dealers. Because *Newsreel* had a somewhat limited circulation, old copies of it are hard to find even in libraries, but any collector new to the field is urged to locate back issues for his own enjoyment and edification.

Serious autograph collectors also should join the Manuscript Society, "an international society established to foster the greater use of original manuscript source material in the study, teaching and writing of history; to facilitate the exchange of information and knowledge among researchers, scholars and collectors; to encourage the meeting together of people with a common interest in autographs, and to stimulate and aid them in their various specialties." Founded in 1948, the Manuscript Society has more than 1,200 members

Autographed and inscribed contemporary photograph of Mary Miles Minter, value $50.

throughout the world, including dealers and collectors, and publishes a quarterly journal, *Manuscripts*, as well as organizing national, annual, and regional meetings. For more information on the Manuscript Society, readers should contact Audrey Arellanes, 1206 North Stoneman Avenue, #15, Alhambra, Calif. 91801.

Perhaps a little more popular in orientation than the Manuscript Society is the Universal Autograph Collectors Club (P.O. Box 467, Rockville Centre, N.Y. 11571), which was founded in 1965 and has more than a thousand members. The U.A.C.C. publishes the bimonthly journal, *The Pen and Quill* and also organizes occasional meetings. The definitive volume on the subject is *Collecting Autographs & Manuscripts* by Charles Hamilton (University of Oklahoma Press, 1974). Hamilton is probably America's best-known autograph dealer and the catalogs for his bimonthly auctions are well worth acquiring, if for no other reason than research into the field. The December, 1982, catalog featured such memorable items as a collection of fourteen letters, written between 1973 and 1982, by the celebrated German filmmaker, Leni Riefenstahl, along with more mundane material, including a lot of twenty-three signed postcards of popular actors and actresses of the Thirties. The Hamilton auctions take place at the New York Sheraton Hotel and the business address is 200 West Fifty-Seventh Street, New York, N.Y. 10019/212-245-7313.

Charles Hamilton's West Coast equivalent is the Scriptorium (427 North Canon Drive, Beverly Hills, Calif. 90210/213-275-6060). Other California-based autograph dealers specializing in motion picture items include B. and B. Nostalgia (14621 East Poulter Drive, Whittier, Calif. 90604/213-941-8309) and Frederick M. Evans (3301 South Bear Street, #44E, Santa Ana, Calif. 92704/714-979-9387).

The best source for film-related autographs used to be Neale Lanigan Autographs (62 Ramsgate Court, Blue Bell, Pa. 19422/215-825-8667), whose listings always featured a number of rare items. Of late, Lanigan's lists have been few and far between and contained little of great excitement. A recent list included signed 8 by 10 photographs of Constance Bennett ($25), Bing Crosby ($50), and Basil Rathbone ($85). Neale Lanigan was co-editor of what is unquestionably the best research tool for authenticating autographs and checking price ranges, *Film Autographs 1894-1941* (published in 1978 and now out of print).

Lanigan's co-editor on the project was James Camner, who operates La Scala Autographs (P.O. Box 268, Plainsboro, N.J. 08536/609-799-8523). As its title suggests, La Scala is chiefly concerned with autographs of opera and musical stars, but most listings contain some film or theatre personalities. A recent catalog included

Autographed photograph of Mary Astor, signed in 1932, value $20.

8 by 10 signed photographs of James Cagney ($35), Frank Capra ($40), Gene Kelly and Frank Sinatra together in *Anchors Aweigh* ($75), and Laurence Olivier ($75).

Aside from Neale Lanigan, the only exclusively film-related autograph dealer who appears to send out regular listings is Jerry S. Redlich (3201 S.W. Fourth Street, Miami, Fla. 33135/305-442-8538). Recent items offered by Redlich have included a 1937 signed Christmas card from Montgomery Clift ($200), an 8 by 10 inscribed still of Alan Ladd in *This Gun for Hire* ($40), a scene from *The Eddy Duchin Story* signed by both Tyrone Power and Kim Novak ($75), and a 1941, 8 by 10 inscribed portrait of Norma Shearer ($35).

There are, of course, many general autograph dealers who list film-related items in their catalogs, and the following is a select list with examples of recent items offered.

Monetary Investment, Ltd. (400 West Silver Spring Drive, Dept. A/P.O. Box 17246, Milwaukee, Wis. 53217/414-961-7005). A typed letter from Ina Claire ($20), an inscribed photograph from Bette Davis ($40), and a 1955 agreement signed by Frank Sinatra ($120).

Robert A. LeGresley (P.O. Box 1455, Henderson, Ky. 42420/502-827-8320). An 8 by 10 portrait of Francis X.

A particularly stunning portrait of Maurice Chevalier and his wife, Yvonne, signed by both, value $75.

Photograph of Brian Aherne and Marlene Dietrich, signed by both, value $75.

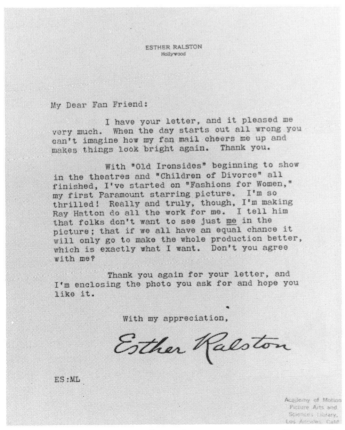

An example of a typical printed response sent to fans in the Twenties and Thirties.

The script for *David Copperfield* (1935), signed by the cast and crew, value $1,500.

Bushman signed in the Fifties ($60), Wallace Beery ink signature ($70), Charlie Chaplin 1921 ink signature ($75), a 1942, 3 by 4 signed photograph of Clark Gable ($170), and an 8 by 10 portrait of Buster Keaton ($65).

The Autograph Alcove (16907 W. North Avenue, Wauwatosa, Wis. 43213/414-271-4304). A 1958 letter from Stan Laurel with interesting content ($225), a 1948 letter from Ronald Reagan with interesting content ($3,000), a contract signed by Merle Oberon ($22.50), a signed 8 by 10 still of Douglas Fairbanks in *The Three Musketeers* ($110), a signed color photograph of Carmen Miranda ($150), W.C. Fields' signature ($150), William S. Hart's signature ($50), a cover of *Life* magazine for April 7, 1952, signed by Marilyn Monroe ($595), original 20 by 26 cards used by guests on *What's My Line* in the mid-Seventies for signing in purposes ($10 each).

Searle's Autographs (P.O. Box 630, St. Marys, Ga. 31558/912-882-5036). An 8 by 10 portrait of Milton Sills ($40), a 1949 letter from Shirley Temple ($75), 8 by 10 portrait of Bette Davis ($12), 8 by 10 portrait of Annabella ($10), pencil signature of Al Jolson ($25).

Robert F. Batchelder (1 West Butler Avenue, Ambler, Pa. 19002/215-643-1430). A 1955 postcard from Bing Crosby ($30), a 1946 agreement signed by Lionel Barrymore ($75), a 1941, 8 by 10 of Ed Wynn ($45), a 1960 signature of Walt Disney on a booklet about Disneyland ($225), a typewritten, one-page letter from Leslie Howard, dated 1921 ($85).

George Houle (2277 Westwood Boulevard, Los Angeles, Calif. 90064/213-474-1539). A typed letter, dated January 22, 1943, signed by Greta Garbo and framed with a photograph ($1,600), a 1959 letter from Jimmy Durante ($32.50), an inscribed copy of Cab Calloway's autobiography, *Of Minnie the Moocher and Me* ($30).

In addition to specialists in the field, autographs can usually be found at many film bookshops and at dealers in lobby cards and posters. A good British source for autographed material is A. & C. Reuter Autographs (64 Spencer Road, Mitcham, Surrey, England). This is the best place to find signed photographs (particularly postcards) of British personalities such as Gracie Fields, Jessie Matthews, and Anna Neagle.

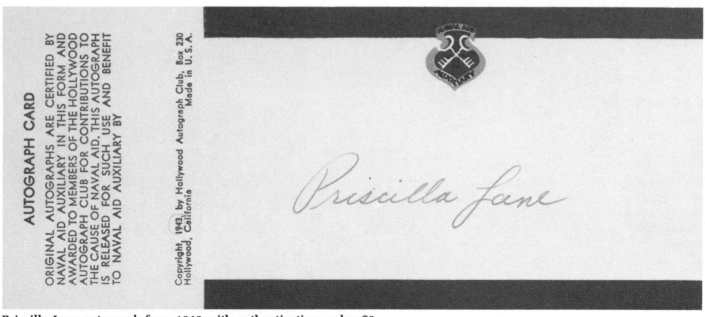

Priscilla Lane autograph from 1943 with authentication, value $6.

3 Films

Of all hobbies associated with the motion picture at the present time, none is more complex than that of collecting films. With the video revolution taking place, more and more people are acquiring videotapes and disks of both old and new feature films. These movies will never increase in value, and, with the limited life of videotape at this time, it is almost certain they will decrease. However, with videotapes and disks so reasonably priced, very few collectors would consider acquiring standard or super 8mm versions of their favorite films at $150 or more a feature when the video version is available at $50 or less.

The 8mm is just one of the film gauges on which films are available. Theatrical feature-length films generally are shot on 35mm (and sometimes "blown up" to 70mm). When these films are released non-theatrically, meaning for home use or for screening at such non-commercial locations as hospitals, prisons, schools, and other institutions, they are reduced to 16mm. For audiences in the home, the films are reduced still further to 8mm, which is divided up into standard 8mm (the old format, now basically defunct) and super 8mm (introduced by Eastman Kodak a few years ago to replace standard). There are a few collectors who specialize in 35mm, but most collectors are interested in 16mm or 8mm. Additionally, there were a number of other substandard gauges popular in Europe, namely 28mm, 17.5mm, and 9.5mm, all introduced by the French-based Pathe Company and all having small numbers of devoted followers.

Aside from the advent of video, film collecting is complicated by the question of its legality. Under American copyright laws, many films are considered "in the public domain," meaning no one actually owns the copyright on them, and they may be sold, copied, and exchanged freely. The copyright owners of some films have made arrangements with legitimate dealers to sell 16mm or 8mm prints of a number of their titles. Many film collectors concern themselves only with these two categories, but there is also a third: films that are still protected by copyright but which find their way into the hands of collectors because prints that were intended to be destroyed by a producer were not. Other films fall into this category because prints were copied or "duped" by unauthorized individuals, or generally because a television distributor leased a package of 16mm prints to a certain television station for so many years and when that lease expired failed to retrieve the films, which were subsequently sold or given away by the station.

With the two exceptions discussed earlier, film producers and distributors maintain that their films are never sold, only leased, and that collectors have no right to own a print of a copyrighted film. But the legal situation here is very confused because collectors have argued somewhat successfully that if they acquire a film by a legitimate means (such as from a television station) and screen it only at their homes for the enjoyment of themselves and their friends, they are making no commercial use of such film, they are taking no profits away from the legitimate owner, and no one is being hurt by their actions.

It is a difficult situation, and has resulted in FBI agents, representing film companies, entering the homes of supposedly law-abiding citizens and seizing films, some of which were acquired perfectly legitimately. Therefore, newcomers to this field are strongly advised to restrict their hobby to purchasing films only from bona-fide dealers. If a fellow collector offers you a film, the copyright status of which concerns you, it is a fairly simple matter to have the Library of Congress conduct a copyright search. Send a fee of $10 with the title of the film and the names of the possible copyright owners to the Registrar of Copyright, The Library of Congress, Washington, D.C. 20559. Unfortunately, it can take up to three months for the Library of Congress to respond. There is an easier—if not definitive—way to check if a film is in the public domain. All films produced during the golden age of the cinema—in other words, prior to 1949—are subject to the rules of the old copyright law, requiring the film's copyright owner to renew the copyright twenty-eight years after the film was first released. An enterprising Los Angeles publisher, Seven Arts Press (6253 Hollywood Boulevard, Hollywood, Calif. 90028), has taken the first three volumes of the Library of Congress copyright catalog, covering the years 1894-1912, 1912-1939, and 1940-1949 and marked each entry to show whether the copyright had been renewed. Seven Arts Press has reprinted those three catalogs, with the company's comments, as *Film Superlist: 20,000 Motion Pictures in the Public Domain* by Jerry Minus and William Storm Hale and *Film Superlist for 1940-1949: Motion Pictures in the U.S. Public Domain* by Walter E. Hurst and William Storm Hale.

There are a surprising number of classic American motion pictures in the public domain and thus available to collectors. Film buffs can now enjoy in the quiet of their own homes such films as *The Birth of a Nation* (1915), *Intolerance* (1916), *Broken Blossoms* (1919), *The Thief of Bagdad* (1924), *Tumbleweeds* (1925), *The Lost World* (1925), *The Phantom of the Opera* (1925), *The Gold Rush* (1925), *The General* (1927), *Of Human Bondage* (1934), *Meet John Doe* (1941), *It's a Wonderful Life* (1946), and *Life with Father* (1947). However, many films are not—and never will be—available to collectors, and there is no point in dreaming of legitimately acquiring prints of *Gone with the Wind*, *The Wizard of Oz*, *The Jazz Singer*, *Casablanca*, or any of the Walt Disney classics.

The major problem facing collectors is print quality. One distributor may have a beautiful 35mm original print of a film, make a new 16mm negative from it, and sell high quality prints struck directly from the 16mm negative. However, because this film is in the public domain, there is absolutely nothing to stop an unscrupulous dealer from making a 16mm negative from a 16mm print acquired from the first dealer and then selling 16mm prints made from that inferior negative. The process can go even further, and a third dealer can purchase one of the inferior 16mm prints and make even another negative. Sadly, the people who suffer are the unwary collectors and the first dealer, who took care to offer high quality prints.

Tumbleweeds (1925), with William S. Hart.

Blood and Sand (1922), with Rudolph Valentino and Nita Naldi.

There is no simple solution to the problem; it is mainly a matter of collectors knowing which dealers to trust and which to bypass. One source of information can be *Classic Images,* which began life as *Classic Film Collector,* and which provides enthusiasts with a wealth of information on the hobby. Under the editorship of its founder, Sam Rubin, this monthly newspaper-type periodical offers news items on subjects related to film history, information on new releases from the dealers, articles of interest to collectors, technical tips, and book reviews. *Classic Images* is published by the Muscatine Journal, a division of Lee Enterprises at P.O. Box 809, Muscatine, IA 52761. Back issues and sample copies are available.

Another newspaper-type journal available to film collectors is *The Big Reel,* now in its ninth year of publica-

Intolerance (1916).

tion. *The Big Reel* (Drawer B, Summerfield, N.C. 27358) is published monthly and is chiefly of interest for the pages and pages of advertisements from collectors selling anything from one 16mm feature to an entire library of films.

In addition to *Classic Images*, Iowa is also the home of Blackhawk Films (1235 West Fifth Street, Davenport, Ia. 52808/319-323-9736), the best known of all companies specializing in films on 16mm, 8mm, and, more recently, videotape and disk for the collector. Blackhawk Films was founded in 1939 by Kent D. Eastin and must take some of the credit for the revival of interest in silent films, particularly silent comedies. The company is exclusive distributor of many of the great Hal Roach comedies, including the Laurel and Hardy features and shorts and the "Our Gang" series. In addition, collec-

tors will find in its one hundred-page quarterly catalog such delights as the best quality prints available on many of the Charlie Chaplin shorts from 1913–19; Charlie Chase, Harry Langdon, and Buster Keaton comedies; documentaries as old as Robert Flaherty's *Nanook of the North* (1922) and as recent as Patrick Montgomery's *Georges Méliès: Cinema Magician* (1978); the Paul Killiam and Saul Turrell series of *Silents Please/The History of the Motion Picture*; Rudolph Valentino in *Blood and Sand* (1922); plus equipment, books, and slides.

In the last category may be found reproductions of original glass slides used in theatres during the silent era, not only to request the audience to be quiet or to be patient while the projectionist changed reels but to suggest that ladies remove their hats. They also

Of Human Bondage (1934), with Reginald Denny, Bette Davis, and Leslie Howard.

announced coming attractions as the forerunners to preview trailers, which came into their own in the Twenties and are still a staple of movie entertainment today. Original glass slides can still be found, usually in antique shops rather than in film-oriented bookshops, and at prices ranging from $10 to $20 apiece.

Blackhawk Films is, of course, only one of more than fifty distributors of films for the private collector. Other recommended dealers include Festival Films (2841 Irving Avenue South, Minneapolis, Minn. 55408/612-822-2680); Glenn Photo Supply (6924 Canby Avenue, Suite 103, Reseda, Calif. 91335/213-981-5506); Griggs-Moviedrome (263 Harrison Street, Nutley, N.J. 07110/201-667-8531); National Cinema Service (Box 43, Ho-Ho-Kus, N.J. 07423/201-445-0776); Reel Images (Box 137, Monroe, Conn. 06468/800-243-0987); and Tamarelle's French Film House (110 Cohasset Stage Road, Chico, Calif. 95926/916-895-3429).

To discover what distributor has what films, it is not always necessary to obtain a catalog. James L. Limbacher's *Feature Films on 8mm, 16mm, and Videotape,* now in its seventh edition, may be an expensive buy at $65 from its publisher, R.R. Bowker (1180 Avenue of the Americas, New York, N.Y. 10036), but is is also a unique publication. As its subtitle indicates, it is ''a directory of feature films available for rental, sale, and lease in the United States and Canada.'' There is a similar volume covering all video releases, both features and shorts, and that is *The Video Source Book,* containing some 1,529 pages, and published by the National Video Clearinghouse, Inc. (100 Lafayette Drive, Syosset, N.Y. 11791). Video collectors should also be aware of an excellent paperback volume that discusses everything one might want to know on the subject, Leonard Maltin and Allan Greenfield's *The Complete Guide to Home Video,* published by Harmony Books.

The Third Man (1949), with Orson Welles.

Broken Blossoms (1919), with Lillian Gish.

4 Magazines

Film magazines can be divided into two basic categories: those aimed at the fans, be they serious or gossipy, and those published for people within the industry. The best known of the trade papers today are *The Hollywood Reporter*, which is published Monday-through-Friday and first appeared in 1930, and *Variety*, which has been published in a daily, Monday-through-Friday edition since 1933 and in a weekly edition since 1905. Both *The Hollywood Reporter* and *Daily Variety* seem to hold little interest for the collector, and back issues from the Thirties sell for little more than $5. The weekly edition of *Variety* is more popular, particularly its annual editions. They boast several hundred pages and are valued at $10. The early weekly *Variety* was published on quality paper, while editions from the Thirties onwards were not, and as these early issues feature fascinating material, not only on film but also on the stage and vaudeville, they are generally priced at $15 each.

The best known of early trade papers is *The Moving Picture World*, published from 1907 through 1928, and single issues of this periodical now sell for around $15 each. The same price will also purchase copies of *Motion Picture News* (which began publication in 1908), *Motography, Exhibitor's Trade Review*, and other half-forgotten early trade publications. Despite the fairly reasonable price for many of these magazines, it should be stressed that it is becoming more and more difficult to find substantial quantities of any of them, and all will prove to be good investments. Even more scarce are copies of what was America's first trade paper, *Views and Film Index*, which began publication in 1906 and later changed its name to *The Film Index*. Single issues of this trade paper could easily sell for $20 or more, as could early issues of such British trade papers as *The*

Kinematograph Weekly and *The Bioscope*, which are almost unheard of in this country.

Closely related to the trade papers are the house organs published by individual producers or distributors to promote their films and contract stars. Among those from 1913-1919 and the Twenties are *The Edison Kinetogram, Vitagraph Life Portrayals, Essanay News, Kalem Kalendar, Lubin Bulletin, The Triangle, Film Follies* (published by the Christie Comedy Company), *Reel Life* (published by Mutual), *The Implet*, and *The Universal Weekly*. Single issues of any of these journals are extremely difficult to find, but perhaps because interest in this period of film history is not that substantial, they generally sell for $10 or less each. Priced considerably higher are similar publications from the Thirties such as *The RKO Flash, Columbia Mirror*, and M-G-M's *The Lion's Roar*. The last can fetch $20 or more when it contains material on popular titles such as *Gone with the Wind, The Wizard of Oz*, or the Jeanette MacDonald-Nelson Eddy features.

Another example of a trade-oriented periodical would be any of the government-sponsored publications produced by individual countries in an effort to sell their product abroad. France, the U.S.S.R., Bulgaria, Romania, and Finland are just a few countries that publish such magazines. As far as collectors are concerned, they are of absolutely no interest, and despite some reference value are almost worthless from a monetary viewpoint.

The periodicals that are most sought by collectors are the fan magazines such as *Photoplay, Motion Picture Classic*, and *Shadowland*. The first fan magazine was titled *The Motion Picture Story Magazine* and was

Moving Picture World, November 10, 1917, the best known of early trade papers, value $15.

THE Universal Weekly

CLEO MADISON
IN
"THE MYSTERY WOMAN"
101 BISON TWO REEL DRAMA
VOL.6 NO. NEW YORK CITY, JAN. 23 1915 PRICE 5 CENTS

An early issue of *The Universal Weekly*, Value $10.

PHOTOPLAY
MAGAZINE

In
This
Issue

*of the World's
Greatest Motion
Picture Publication*

The Movie
Broadway
By RENNOLD WOLF

The Picture Bat-
tle in Congress

*THREE GREAT
SHORT STORIES*

Art Portraits
Personality Stories
Photoplay Criticisms
Plays and Players

Edna
Mayo

*April
15 Cents*

A 1916 issue of *Photoplay*, value $10.

33

MOVING PICTURE STORIES

February 18, 1930
Vol. 36, No. 841

10¢

Helen Twelvetrees
PATHÉ

Lonely?
Join Rosemary
Lee's Helping
Hearts Club

The Grand Parade
The Bishop Murder Case
It's a Great Life
Mexicali Rose

A typical Thirties cheaply produced fan magazine, *Moving Picture Stories*, value $10.

The cover of the February, 1923, issue of *Motion Picture Classic,* value $12.

A cover from an issue of Britain's best fan magazine of the silent era, *Picturegoer,* value $10.

founded in February of 1911 by Eugene V. Brewster and J. Stuart Blackton. It was followed a few months later by *Photoplay,* which was to become the best known of all fan magazines, rightly subtitled "The National Movie Magazine." In their early years, both periodicals contained little other than fictionalized versions of current films, and it really took a couple of years before they began featuring articles on contemporary personalities. By then *The Motion Picture Story Magazine* had become known simply as *Motion Picture Magazine.*

Yet again because of a general lack of interest from many collectors, copies of these and other early fan magazines can sell for as little as $8 each. Indeed, in pricing most magazines, it is not so much the content as the celebrity on the cover that determines the price. A typical fan magazine from the Twenties or Thirties may be worth only $10 a copy, but should it have Valentino, Joan Crawford, Claudette Colbert, or Clark Gable on its cover the price can go as high as $15. Collectors should not only pay attention to the covers but should also check the contents very carefully to ensure that no page has been removed or that nothing has been clipped. It is surprising how many times one will locate what appears to be a mint copy of a magazine only to discover after unwrapping it from a cellophane covering (often over the protests of the dealer) that a small review or a photograph has been clipped.

Other American fan magazines that are highly collectible include *Movie Weekly, Photo-Play Journal, Motion Picture Classic,* and *Feature Movie Magazine.* One interesting early fan magazine is *Moving Picture Stories,* whose content is so similar to that of *The Universal Weekly* it is very obvious that it was also sponsored by Universal.

Collectors should also be aware of the many British fan magazines. The best was *Film Weekly,* which began publication in 1928 and ceased with the outbreak of World War II in Europe in 1939. Each oversized issue features numerous well-written articles far superior to the usual fan magazine fare. The most popular of the British publications were *Pictures and the Picturegoer* (commonly known simply as *Picturegoer*) and *Picture Show.* The last was always printed on very cheap paper and is not recommended for collectors, but *Picturegoer,* published on a monthly basis in the Twenties, was responsible for a high production quality magazine. If one can locate a copy in this country, it can be valued at $10 to $15. Similar in look and paper quality to *Picture Show* were *Boys Cinema* and *Girls Cinema,* two sexist periodicals that would have feminists up in arms today. They made very careful distinctions between what motion pictures would appeal to a boy and what to a girl. *Boys Cinema* would feature cowboy stars such as William S. Hart, while *Girls Cinema* might reveal Mary Pickford's hobbies or Lillian Gish's devotion to her mother.

Another British fan magazine that is seldom found in this country, but which will become a collector's item because of its unique nature and the quality of its paper, is *ABC Film Review*, published monthly between 1952 and 1972 for sixpence (or twenty-five cents) a copy. The magazine could be purchased only at the ABC cinema chain in Britain, and it was devoted to the films and personalities seen on the ABC circuit. American collectors interested in acquiring British film magazines should check out the British dealers mentioned in the first chapter as well as contacting Treasures and Pleasures (18 Newport Court, London WC2H 7JS) and Vintage Magazine Company, Ltd. (39-41 Brewer Street, London W.1). An American dealer recently sold twelve issues of *Picturegoer* from 1921 for $165, and with the scarcity of this type of periodical in the United States it seems highly probable that price will double two years from now.

Close Up, published between 1927 and 1933, was the first of the serious, or so-called intellectual, film magazines to appear on the scene. Although reprinted at a reasonable price in more recent years by the Arno Press, original copies are quite scarce and sell for $10 each. Similar in style and content to *Close Up* were *Cinema Quarterly*, published in Britain between 1932 and 1935, *Films*, published from 1939-1940, and *Hollywood Quarterly*, which began publication in 1945 and is still going strong today as *Film Quarterly*. In the tradition of *Close Up* are such contemporary American film periodicals as *Film Culture*, *Film Comment*, *Literature/Film Quarterly*, *Cinema Journal*, and *Film Heritage*, all of which are too recent to be valued at anything more than their cover price. *Film Culture* and *Film Comment* are probably the two periodicals that offer the best bet for collecting with a view to a complete set having a high value in a few years. Despite its superficiality, *American Film*, published since October of 1975 by the American Film Institute, appears to have become popular with collectors and early out-of-print issues can sell for upwards of $5. *American Cinematographer*, published by the American Society of Cinematographers, is generally a little too technical to be of interest to most collectors. But the issues devoted to the special effects in such recent films as *Star Wars* and *Star Trek* quickly became collectors' items and, unless reprinted, are going to become very valuable in the future.

Other periodicals worth considering include *Films and Filming*, which began publication in Britain in 1954 and early issues of which sell at $5 each, and *Cinema Papers*, a large format magazine from Australia first published in 1967 and which shows signs of becoming highly collectible. The British Film Institute *Sight and Sound*, first published in 1934, should be more collectible than it is currently, and complete years from the Thirties through the Fifties will one day sell for $50 or

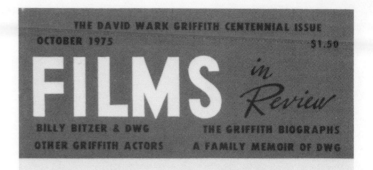

Back issues of *Films in Review* will always be collectible, and those issues still available from the publisher will prove good investments.

Back issues of *Films and Filming* continue to increase in value. This 1961 issue is now valued at $3.

MOTION PICTURE

A BANCROFT PUBLICATION
MOTION PICTURE
10¢

DECEMBER
NSC

CLAUDETTE
COLBERT

BE AN AMERICAN

WHY STIRLING HAYDEN QUIT HOLLYWOOD

Motion Picture for December, 1941, value $15 because of Claudette Colbert's presence on the cover.

GROUP DISCUSSION GUIDE

INCLUDING PHOTOPLAY STUDIES

Copyright 1940 by Educational and Recreational Guides, Inc.

Published monthly, except July and August, by Educational and Recreational Guides, Inc., 1501 Broadway, New York, N. Y. Application for entry as second-class matter is pending.

Volume V, Number 4   APRIL, 1940   25c a copy, 2.00 a year

CLARK GABLE AND VICTOR FLEMING, DIRECTOR OF "GONE WITH THE WIND"

IN THIS ISSUE: GUIDES TO "GONE WITH THE WIND," "SEVENTEEN," "OUR TOWN"

RECOMMENDED BY THE MOTION-PICTURE COMMITTEE OF THE DEPARTMENT OF SECONDARY TEACHERS OF THE NATIONAL EDUCATION ASSOCIATION

An educational magazine popular in the Thirties and Forties, this particular issue of *Group Discussion Guide* features *Gone with the Wind* and hence is valued at $10.

FILM WEEKLY, Friday, September 13, 1935

Registered at the G.P.O. as a Newspaper

THE NATIONAL GUIDE TO FILMS

Film Weekly

3D.

FRIDAY
SEPT 13
1935

THE FULL STORY OF

FREDDIE BARTHOLOMEW

("YOUNG COPPERFIELD")

MAUREEN O'SULLIVAN
and FRANK LAWTON IN
"DAVID COPPERFIELD"

Film Weekly, the best British fan magazine of the Thirties, value $15.

39

more. *Sequence*, published in the late Forties by a group of Oxford University students, and which contains the first critical writings of director Lindsay Anderson, is also highly collectible, as is a set of *Penguin Film Review* from the early Fifties.

For reference alone, another British Film Institute publication, *The Monthly Film Bulletin*, featuring detailed credits, synopses, and commentaries on current films, should be of interest to collectors. And yet bound volumes from the Thirties and Forties sell for as little as $25 a set. Similarly, the American equivalent of *The Monthly Film Bulletin*, *Film Facts*, should also have collectible value in years to come.

The best known of all reference periodicals is *Films in Review*, published by the National Board of Review since February of 1950. It contains detailed career articles and, in the years when it was edited by Henry Hart, vitriolic film reviews. Arno Press has reprinted the first four volumes, but even so, single issues from the Fifties and Sixties can sell for $10 each. A complete set of *Films in Review* has been known to sell for $1,500. Becoming increasingly scarce are two journals similar in content to *Films in Review*: Alan G. Barbour's *Screen Facts* and Leonard Maltin's *Film Fan Monthly*. Larry Edmunds Bookshop has a good stock of *Screen Facts*, with some issues at rather outrageous prices. The major competitor to *Films in Review* was the British *Focus on Film*, first published in January of 1970 and merged with *Films and Filming* in 1981. *Focus on Film* is another periodical that will become increasingly valuable in years to come, and collectors would do well to purchase remaining back issues while they are still available from the publisher, The Tantivy Press (Magdalen House, 136-148 Tooley Street, London SE1 2TT).

The German periodical *Film Kurier* was devoted to pictorial layouts on individual films, and issues from the Thirties, particularly those featuring Nazi films and the features of Lillian Harvey, are eagerly sought at $10 each. The French periodical *Cine Monde* is another featuring fine photographic layouts, and those collectors with a working knowledge of French should also not ignore *Cahiers du Cinéma*, once the most famous of all critical monthlies, and *L'Avant-Scène du Cinéma*, which publishes one complete film script in each issue.

Vanity does not prevent my mentioning a periodical that I edited from 1968 through 1974, *The Silent Picture*. My co-founder Paul O'Dell and I billed it as "The only serious quarterly devoted to the art and history of the silent film." A complete set of all nineteen issues of the journal has been reprinted by Arno Press, but back issues, all of which are long out of print, now sell for $5 or more. Yet again, *The Velvet Light Trap* and the Seattle-based *Movietone News*, are or were produced in such small quantities that they can do nothing but in-

crease in value. A journal such as *Image*, a beautiful quarterly devoted to film and photography and printed on the highest quality art paper, is published by a major film institution, the International Museum of Photography at George Eastman House (900 East Avenue, Rochester, N.Y. 14607), but because its distribution is so poor every issue, even those still in print have become collectors' items.

Non-film magazines can sometimes offer worthwhile issues for collectors. *Life* has published a number of cover stories relating to the cinema, notably Lauren Bacall in its issue of October 16, 1944 (selling for $12.50), Audrey Hepburn in its issue of July 18, 1955 ($7.50), Marilyn Monroe in its issue of August 17, 1962 ($10), and the special Nostalgia issue of February 19, 1971 ($7.50). The new *Life* magazine for February, 1980, featured Mary Astor on its cover in connection with a special photographic essay, "Whatever Became of Mary Astor and Other Lost Stars?" It included photographs of Mary Astor, Louise Brooks, Ina Claire, Frances Dee, Billie Dove, Laura La Plante, Pola Negri, Vera Hruba Ralston, and Loretta Young as they appear today. A collector's item by any standard, this issue of *Life* will become increasingly valuable, particularly if autographed by some of the stars. Before the better known *Life* came into existence in 1936 there was another *Life* magazine devoted to humor. It boasted Robert Sherwood as its film critic in the Twenties and also published at least one special issue devoted to the movies. Also, in Great Britain, *Life* had an imitator in *Picture Post*, which featured cover stories similar to its American competitor. Ernest Betts profiled Charlie Chaplin, "A Great Man Is Sixty," in the April 16, 1949, issue.

There is no accurate record of just how many film periodicals have been published since the cinema began. The number is probably well over a thousand and the library of the British Film Institute boasts holdings of more than eight hundred. All have some value in recording contemporary cinema and documenting film history, and the majority are or will become collector's items.*

---

* Readers interested in learning more about film periodicals should consult essays by this writer: "The Story of the Film Magazine" in *Film Review 1979-1980* (W.H. Allen) and "Early Film Magazines: An Overview" in *Aspects of American Film History prior to 1920* (Scarecrow Press).

WALLACE REID.—Splendid Full-Page Picture Inside.

TWOPENCE.   MAY 8, 1920.

Picture Show

No. 54.   Vol. 3.

BILL HART, the Boys' Idol, Approves of the Real Wild West Adventure Paper, the "Boys' Cinema."

BILL HART Edits a page in the "BOYS' CINEMA" each week.   This work he explains how to light signal fires and send messages by smoke.

Picture Show, a cheaply produced British fan magazine, value $10.

5 Still Photographs

Just as a signed original portrait of a star is worth far more than a signed copy portrait, so an original photographic still is worth more than a recent copy, no matter how good that copy. The only exception is when a new print is made from the original negative rather than from a copy negative of an original print. It is not too difficult even for the untrained eye to spot the difference, but it is a situation that seldom arises because few original still negatives seem to have survived, and those that have are not generally accessible to dealers or collectors.

Still photographs are posed pictures taken on the set during or immediately before or after the filming of a scene. They are usually of a sequence—a dramatic or comic moment—from the film, but may also show the production staff—the director, producer, cameraman, etc.—at work or the players relaxing prior to a take, reading the script or rehearsing. Portrait or candid photographs of the stars are, of course, taken at special sessions and generally not on the set. These portrait photographs are usually retouched—skin blemishes, bags under the eyes, wrinkles, and double chins are painted out. Occasionally one will come across a photograph with a black mark across it, indicating that the star or a representative has rejected it for publicity purposes and the shot has been "killed." Sometimes the photograph will have small marks across the face of the subjects, indicating where retouching is necessary. It is always somewhat disquieting to find an unretouched photograph and discover that one's favorite actress has hairy legs or the beginnings of a double chin.

In addition to still photographs, there are frame enlargements, which are precisely that—photographs enlarged directly from the 35mm frame of the motion picture film. Such frame enlargements are generally grainy or blurred. Frame enlargements sometimes double as publicity stills when a feature film has been produced fairly cheaply and without a still photographer on the set. Although frame enlargements are preferred by many film scholars for illustrative purposes because they show the scene exactly as it appeared in the film, they are generally shunned by collectors for being somewhat lacking in glamor and photographic quality.

No one knows when the first still photograph was taken. Certainly, as early as 1907 both the Edison and Vitagraph Companies were using stills (as opposed to frame enlargements) to publicize their films. There is no exact date as to when eight inches by ten inches became the standard size for still photographs. Early in the century many photographs were five inches by seven inches. In those early days, most stills were printed on what is called double-weight matt paper, being, as the description suggests, double the weight of the paper used for today's stills and not dried "glossy." As a consequence, many stills from the silent era have a sturdy feel to them. One holds something of substance, a feeling one does not receive from today's flimsy and often poorly posed stills. Of course, one of the main reasons for the better quality of earlier stills was the use of 8 by 10 negatives, along with the photographer's concern for careful lighting and posing. The lack of these techniques today will often explain the grainy appearance of contemporary stills.

In the silent era, Evans, Hartsook, and Witzel were three major Los Angeles-based photographers responsible for many of the portrait photographs of the stars released by the various studios for publicity purposes. In the Twenties, Melbourne Spurr and Lansing Brown

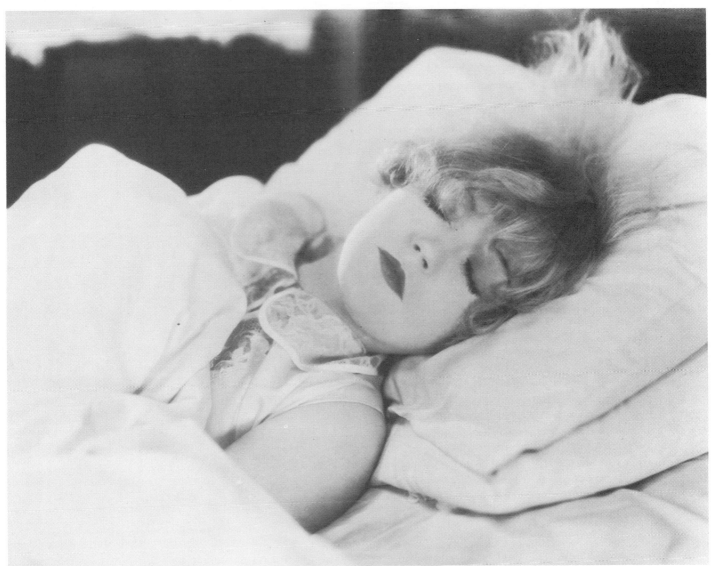

Marion Davies in the unreleased *The 5 O'Clock Girl.*

joined the photographic fraternity, and some studios began using staff photographers. M-G-M boasted Clarence Sinclair Bull and George Hurrell, while Universal had Roman Freulich. Karl Struss began his illustrious career in the film industry as a still photographer for Cecil B. DeMille. Original photographs by both Struss and Hurrell prove good hedges against inflation and, when signed, are valued in the hundreds of dollars, particularly now that Struss is dead and Hurrell will not sign any "old" photographs. For further information on both men, readers should consult *Karl Struss: Man with a Camera* (Cranbrook Academy of Art/Museum, 1976) and *The Hurrell Style,* with text by Whitney Stine (John Day Company, 1976).

Poorly reproduced photographs by both Bull and Freulich can be found in *The Faces of Hollywood: Clarence Sinclair Bull* (A.S. Barnes, 1968) and *Forty Years in Hollywood: Roman Freulich* (A.S. Barnes, 1971). But beautiful reproductions of the work of

Hollywood photographers are included in *The Image Makers* by Richard Lawton, with a text by Paul Trent (McGraw-Hill, 1972), and *Grand Illusions* by Richard Lawton, with a text by Hugo Leckey (McGraw-Hill, 1973). First editions of both are collector's items. The best overview of the still photographer's art in the cinema is the sumptuously illustrated *The Art of the Great Hollywood Portrait Photographers, 1925-1940* by John Kobal (Alfred A. Knopf, 1980).

As early as June 4, 1939, The *New York Times* announced that "collecting old stills is the latest pastime of California connoisseurs," noting that some forty original stills from *The Birth of a Nation* were sold that year for $100. (That same set today would be worth well over $1,000.) Obviously, what an individual collects depends purely on personal preference. There are some collectors who will take any still photograph, but the majority specialize in scene stills or portraits, silent or sound, Academy Award winners, cheesecake or beef-

MARY PICKFORD
"The World's Sweetheart"
FAMOUS PLAYERS' LEADING ARTISTE
CONTROLLED BY J.D. WALKER'S WORLD'S FILMS LTD

A British Mary Pickford postcard, circa 1915, value $5.

A marvelous 1941 photograph titled "Hays Office Rejects," illustrating everything which the film industry at that time could not depict in a still photograph.

Roy D'Arcy and Renee Adoree in their uncompleted 1928 version of *Rose Marie*.

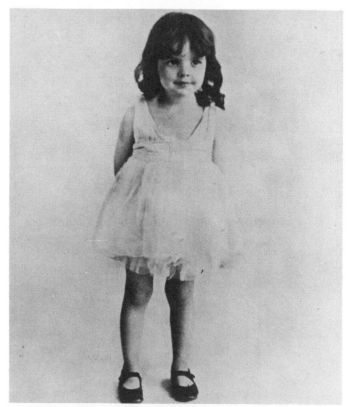

Childhood photographs of stars, such as this one of Judy Garland, are eagerly sought. Happily many studios did release such photographs, and originals can be worth from $5 each.

Sherlock Holmes proves a good subject for stills collectors. Here we see some of the more famous Sherlock Holmes of the screen: Eille Norwood, John Barrymore, Arthur Wontner, Basil Rathbone, and Clive Brook.

A still from the French version of the 1931 Laurel and Hardy feature, *Pardon Us,* in which Boris Karloff replaced Walter Long.

A 1915 Charlie Chaplin postcard, value $6.

cake, musicals or comedies, or a specific star or group of stars. As with any area of film-related collectibles, the highest priced items are always those most popular, such as original portrait stills of Al Jolson, Judy Garland, Humphrey Bogart, Marlene Dietrich, Rudolph Valentino, and Clara Bow. Particularly rare are original Greta Garbo stills, especially from her Swedish films (which are just about unique in this country), or from the 1930 German-language version of *Anna Christie,* which boasted not only a different cast and director from the English-language version, but also a different makeup for the star. Other rarities are scenes cut from films or shots of players who were subsequently replaced by others, such as Beulah Bondi (replaced by Bodil Rosing) in *The Painted Veil* (1934), ZaSu Pitts (replaced by Beryl Mercer) in *All Quiet on the Western Front* (1930), and Renée Adorée (replaced by Joan Crawford) in *Rose Marie* (1928). Even rarer are stills from films that, for one reason or another, were never released. These include the 1931 Marie Dressler M-G-M musical, *March of Time,* and the abortive Marion Davies feature, *The 5 O'Clock Girl.* Also rare are stills "killed" or rejected by the Hays Office as unsuitable publicity materials.

In addition to still photographs, many collectors specialize in postcards. Typical are the series of colored shots of movie star homes issued from the early days onwards, and portraits of celebrities, more prevalent in Europe than this country. Postcard shows are held regularly throughout the country, and almost every postcard dealer offers a sampling of film-related cards. More obscure are stamps, not only those officially produced by the Postal Service to honor events such as the D.W. Griffith centenary (1975), the fiftieth anniversary of talking pictures (1977), and the one hundredth anniversary of the birth of Will Rogers (1979), but such novelty items as a set of forty-eight stamps of Warner Bros. stars produced as a giveaway in theatres during 1935. First-day covers are becoming highly praised, and will eventually become valuable collectors' items. Collectors should also investigate postage stamps issued abroad, including the French stamps honoring Georges Méliès and the Lumiere brothers.

Two major research libraries in the United States possess collections numbering many millions of stills, and any can be copied at a reasonable fee. These are the Museum of Modern Art (11 West Fifty-Third Street, New York, N.Y. 10019) and the Academy of Motion Picture Arts and Sciences (8949 Wilshire Boulevard, Beverly Hills, Calif. 90211). In addition, the British Film Institute (81 Dean Street, London W1V 6AA) operates a major stills library, and, unlike its American counterparts, the Institute has a published catalog of its holdings (compiled by Markku Salmi and produced in paperback format in 1982). *Catalogue of Stills, Poster and Designs* lists over thirty-seven thousand titles of films from all over the world produced between 1895 and 1981, and

A postcard photograph of Rudolph Valentino, originally issued by the British periodical, *Picturegoer,* value $5.

stills, posters, and designs for all are held by the British Film Institute.

Two semi-private sources are also worth investigating. For photographs of Hollywood locations, from streets to studios, Pacific Federal Savings and Loan Association (6801 Hollywood Boulevard, Hollywood, Calif. 90028/213-463-4141) is the best source, boasting a collection of more than ten thousand photographs. Illustrating the history of Hollywood back to 1884, they are under the care of its senior vice-president, Bruce Torrence. Marc Wanamaker operates the Bison Archives (1600 Schuyler Road, Beverly Hills, Calif. 90210/213-275-3624), which holds more than forty thousand stills illustrating the history of the motion picture industry from behind the scenes. The Bison Archives is the place to check for photographs of obscure film studios, and its copies sell for between $5 and $10 each.

There are very few second-hand bookshops in America that do not have some still photographs for sale. The

Director Jacques Feyder, Greta Garbo, Herman Bing, and Salka Viertel on the set of the 1930 German-language version of *Anna Christie*.

two leading film book specialists, Cinemabilia (10 West Thirteenth Street, New York, N.Y. 10011), and Larry Edmunds Bookshop (6658 Hollywood Boulevard, Hollywood, Calif. 90028), both have good selections of photographs that are broken down by films and personalities. Edmunds generally charges $2 for a copy and up to $12 for an original.

The best collection of stills for sale on the West Coast is that of Eddie Brandt's Saturday Matinee (6310 Colfax Avenue, P. O. Box 3232, North Hollywood, Calif. 91609/ 213-506-4242), which modestly states that it has "the world's second-largest collection of stills." Eddie Brandt's is the place to locate rare and unusual stills dating back to early in the century, as well as photographs of theatre, radio, and television personalities, posters, lobby cards, and press books. Copy stills and recent stills sell for $1.50 each, while originals from an earlier vintage average $5.

Douglas J. Hart (7279-A Sunset Boulevard,

Hollywood, Calif. 90046/213-876-6070) is located in an alley off Sunset Boulevard and is open on Saturdays only, but this shop is crammed with hundreds of thousands of stills, all arranged by film or personality. The emphasis is more on recent products, although Hart does maintain a good selection of Hal Roach-related stills. Chapman's Picture Palace (1757 North Las Palmas, Hollywood, Calif. 90028/213-467-1739) offers a good selection of stills with particular emphasis on color photographs of more popular personalities such as Marilyn Monroe and Judy Garland. Proprietor Bob Chapman also possesses a number of negatives of M-G-M stars photographed by Clarence Sinclair Bull, and copies are available at a reasonable rate.

For reasonably priced copy photographs (no originals) collectors should sent want lists to Quality First (c/o 6546 Hollywood Boulevard, Suite 201, Hollywood, Calif. 90028). Other Los Angeles-based stills outlets worth exploring include Bond Street Books (1638 North Wilcox Avenue, Hollywood, Calif. 90028/213-464-8060) which has some sorted stills available at $2 each, and also offers hundreds of thousands of unsorted stills at 20 cents each. If one has the patience, it is possible to find a bargain. Similar buys can be found at the Burbank Book Castle (200 North Golden Mall, Burbank, Calif. 91502/213-845-1563). Collectors Book Store, also known as Bennett's (6763 Hollywood Boulevard, Hollywood, Calif. 90028/213-467-3296), offers a large selection of stills priced from $1.50 to $12.50. All are meticulously filed, but the sales staff has little enthusiasm for collectors who check more than one file without purchasing anything. In addition to stills, Collectors Book Store offers posters (including some beautiful one-sheets from the silent era at very reasonable prices), comic books, scripts, and novelty items.

In New York the most famous of all stills outlets is Movie Star News (212 East Fourteenth Street/P.O. Box 191, New York, N.Y. 10276/212-777-5564 and 212-982-8364). Now operated by Paula Klaw, Movie Star News was established by her late husband, Irving Klaw, described by the *New York Times* (November 16, 1947) as the undisputed "King of Pin-Ups" and "King of Movie Stills." Movie Star News has literally millions

of stills, arranged by film and personality, and operates a thriving mail order business. Its twenty-eight page, well-illustrated catalog, which is available for $1, lists thousands of photographs broken down by movie scenes, popular movie star portraits, physique photos, great Westerns, pinup poses, bondage, spanking, and catfight photos. The catalog also lists four pages of press books priced at $10 and up.

Stephen Sally (339 West Forty-Fourth Street/P.O. Box 646, New York, N.Y. 10036/213-246-4972) issues a forty-page catalog of portraits and scene stills for sale at the incredibly low price of $1 each. In addition, Sally also sells 8 by 10 black-and-white photographs of hundreds of film posters at $2 each, and among these one may find *Cimarron* (1931), *It Happened One Night* (1934), *Frankenstein* (1931), and *Hollywood Cavalcade* (1939). Other New York sources of stills are Ludlow Sales (P.O. Box 554, New York, N.Y. 10011) and The Memory Shop (P.O. Box 364, New York, N.Y. 10003/212-473-2404). Collectors should also be aware that many of the dealers mentioned in Chapter 8, Posters and Lobby Cards, also generally have a selection of film stills for sale.

PHOTOPLAY

SEPTEMBER

25¢

JEANETTE MacDONALD

Beginning: **THE CASE OF THE HOLLYWOOD SCANDAL**
A New Murder Mystery Thriller **By ERLE STANLEY GARDNER**
HOW I SAVED MY MARRIAGE By Dorothy Lamour
WHO IS HOLLYWOOD'S SMARTEST HOSTESS? By Cornelius V

Because Jeanette MacDonald is on the cover, this issue of *Photoplay* from the Thirties is valued at $15.

Souvenir program for *Show Boat* (1929), value $20.

A lobby card from the 1939 cult classic, *The Wizard of Oz*, value $1,000.

Because this 1933 lobby card from *Duck Soup* shows all four Marx Brothers together, it is valued at $400.

A lobby card from the only film in which both W.C. Fields and Mae West starred, *My Little Chickadee* (1940), value $150.

A lobby card from the 1948 feature, *Easter Parade*, value $75.

A novelty bridge game item, featuring silent star Dorothy Mackaill, value $5.

Poster for *Hell's Angels* (1930), value $3,000.

Poster for *Frankenstein* (1931), value $5,000.

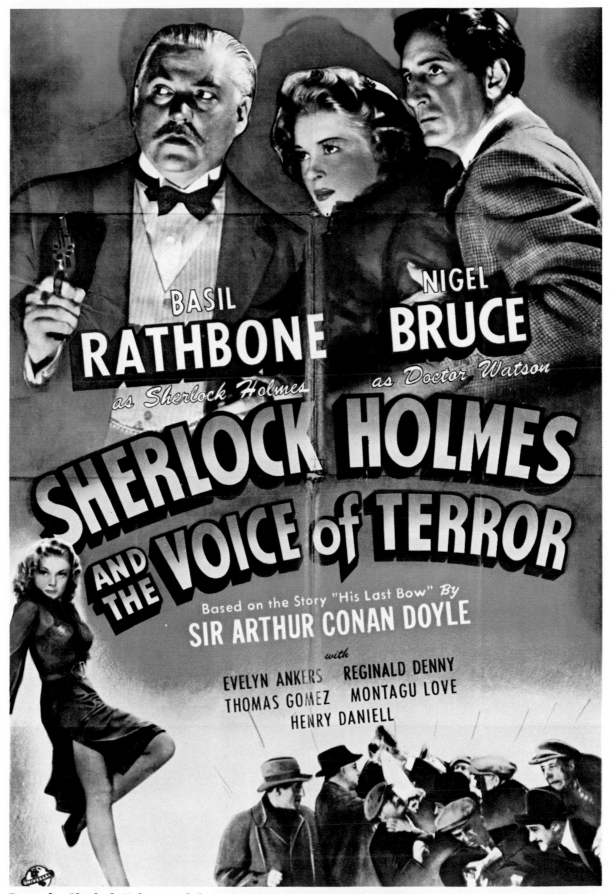

Poster for *Sherlock Holmes and the Voice of Terror* (1942), value $300.

Poster for *Singin' in the Rain* (1952), value $150.

6 Sheet Music

Music has always been an integral part of the motion picture. The earliest film screenings featured some form of musical accompaniment, and by about 1916 all of the major motion picture theatres had orchestras to accompany the silent films in the evening. Usually a piano or an organ sufficed for the matinee performances. Only the smallest of cinema houses had simply a tinkling piano, today's stereotype for silent film music accompaniment. The first music to be specially composed to accompany a silent film is generally believed to have been Camille Saint-Saëns' score, published as his Opus 128 for strings, piano, and harmonium, for the 1908 French film, *L'Assassinat du Duc de Guise/The Assassination of the Duke de Guise*. It was a mere ten minutes (one reel) in length. Probably the first original American composition for the motion picture was Walter Cleveland Simon's score for the 1911 Kalem production, *Arrah-na-Pogue*.

Soon after it became fairly common practice to publish original or specially arranged scores for silent features. In addition, several books or folios of music for film accompaniment were available published by Sam Fox, Schirmer, Photoplay Music, and others. The noted film composer Erno Rapée, who composed the theme song, "Charmaine," for the 1926 feature, *What Price Glory?*, was responsible for two volumes of silent film music: *Moving Picture Moods for Pianists and Organists* (1924) and *Encyclopedia of Music for Pictures* (1925). In addition, "thematic music cue sheets" were circulated in the Twenties. Published by the Cameo Music Publishing Company, these provided the opening bars from appropriate serious or popular music with cues as to titles or action when the accompaniment was to change.

Music cue sheets are becoming scarce, but can still be purchased for an average price of $5 each. Complete scores for silent films are equally rare but, surprisingly, when they do appear on the market they sell fairly cheaply, perhaps because there is little glamor attached to a volume of music devoid of photographs or any colors other than black and white. Scores for Triangle features of the early days have been seen for sale as low as $10 each, while an original score for D.W. Griffith's *Hearts of the World* (1918) was sold in Los Angeles two years ago for $25. At least one piano selection from the score of a silent film has been published with photographs of scenes from the production, and that is by Schirmer from the 1916 Annette Kellermann feature, *A Daughter of the Gods*.

The type of music that most interests movie memorabilia collectors is sheet music featuring a celebrity on the cover. Most collectors buy exclusively for the covers and are unable to read music and appreciate the composer's art. From the Thirties onwards there were few songs from Hollywood musicals that were not available in sheet music form. Albums of sheet music were also published such as *Hollywood Dance Folio*, *The Bill Boyd Song Book*, *Paramount Song Folio*, and *Popular Song Book*, which featured stories on film personalities as well as the lyrics and music to their associated songs. Judy Garland is the most popular cover personality on sheet music followed by Marlene Dietrich and Al Jolson. A good beginner's guide to the subject is *Introducing the Song Sheet* by Helen Westin (Thomas Nelson, 1976).

During the silent era, many songs were published in dedication to a celebrity or boosting a theme song from a contemporary film, all featuring popular silent stars on their covers. There has been much joking about the

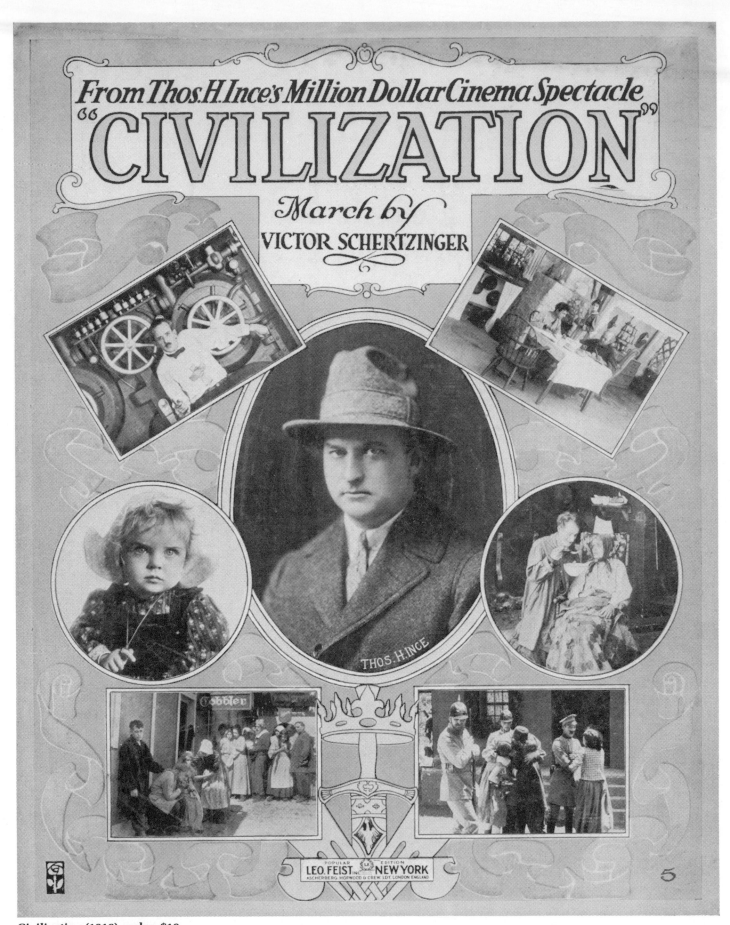

Civilization (1916), value $10.

Sheet music for one of the earliest songs associated with the motion picture, *The Vitagraph Girl,* value $12.

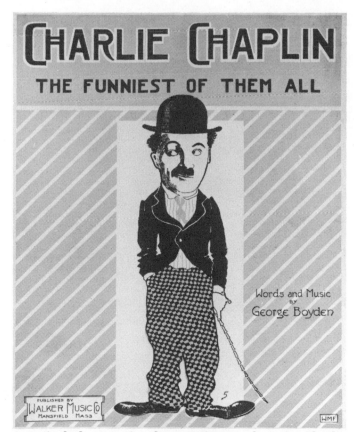

A particularly attractive sheet music cover featuring Charlie Chaplin, dating from 1915, value $15.

title songs from silent films, the funniest supposedly being from the 1928 Norma Talmadge feature, *The Woman Disputed.* Its theme song was "Woman Disputed, I Love You." Equally amusing is the theme song from the 1928 Richard Dix feature, *Redskin,* which was concerned with the pride of native Americans and the efforts of the white race to belittle that pride. The opening line of the theme song "Redskin" is "Redskin, redskin, boy of my dreams." However, as funny as these may be, they are no more amusing than the publishing of a theme song, "Across 110th Street," from the 1972 film of the same name. The movie dealt with a bloody battle between the police and the inhabitants of New York's Spanish Harlem.

There is no complete listing of the number of songs featuring silent film personalities on their covers, and the following is merely a sampling: "Dear Old Daddy Long Legs" (1919, Mary Pickford); "Dolores" (1928, Dolores Del Rio); "I'm Sorry I Made You Cry" (1918, June Elvidge and John Bowers); "Norma" (1919, Norma Talmadge); "Rose of Monterey" (1927, Mary Astor and Gilbert Roland); "Charlie Chaplin the Funniest of Them All" (1915, Charlie Chaplin); "Sweet Little Mary Pickford" (1914, Mary Pickford); "When Romance Wakes" (1923, Corinne Griffith); "Daughter of Mine" (1919, Madge Kennedy); "His Majesty, the American" (1919, Douglas Fairbanks); "Oh, You Delicious Little Devil" (1919, Mae Murray); "Salvation Rose" (1919, Marion Davies); "Come Out of the Kitchen Mary Ann" (1916, Douglas Fairbanks); "After You Went Away" (1919, Vivian Martin); "Days When We Went to School" (1920, Dorothy Gish).

Also, "I'm Forever Blowing Bubbles" (1919, June Caprice); "Bring Back My Daddy to Me" (1917, Madge Evans); "Fallen Idols" (1919, Evelyn Nesbitt); "Sipping Cider thru a Straw" (1919, Roscoe "Fatty" Arbuckle); "Wings of the Morning" (1919, William Farnum); "Please Come Back to Me" (1919, Mabel Normand); "The Red Circle Waltz" (1916, Ruth Roland); "I've Lost You So Why Should I Care" (1916, Theda Bara); "Sweetheart of Mine" (1914, Mary Pickford); "Runaway June" (1915, Norma Phillips); "Just an Old Love Song," the love theme from *Robin Hood* (1922, Douglas Fairbanks); "My Ship o' Dreams" (1915, Francis X. Bushman); "I Love-a Dat Man" (1914, Maurice Costello); "It's Never Too Late To Be Sorry" (1919, Marguerite Snow), and "Oh Helen!" (1918, Roscoe "Fatty" Arbuckle).

Nor should one forget the two popular songs associated with serial queen Pearl White: "Poor Pauline" (1914) from *The Perils of Pauline,* and "Elaine My Moving Picture Queen" (1915) from *The Exploits of Elaine.* The lyrics of Elaine exhorted:

"Elaine, Elaine, please come down from the screen.
"And be my Moving Picture Queen!"

Broken Blossoms (1919), value $20.

Robin Hood (1922), value $20.

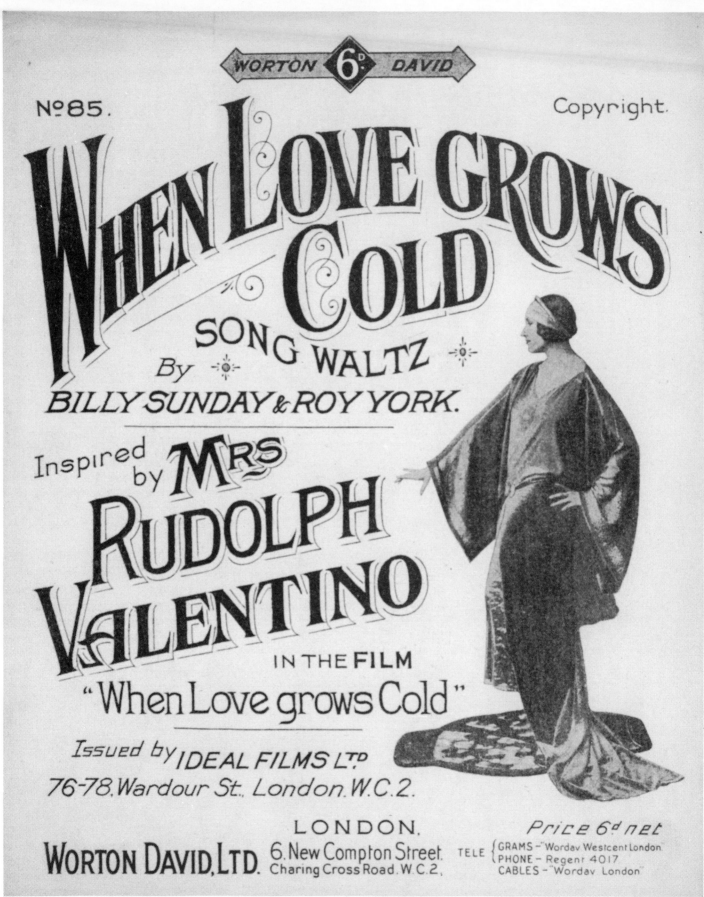

An unusual piece of sheet music exploiting the film *When Love Grows Cold* (1925), which Natacha Rambova in turn used to exploit her separation from husband Valentino, value $15.

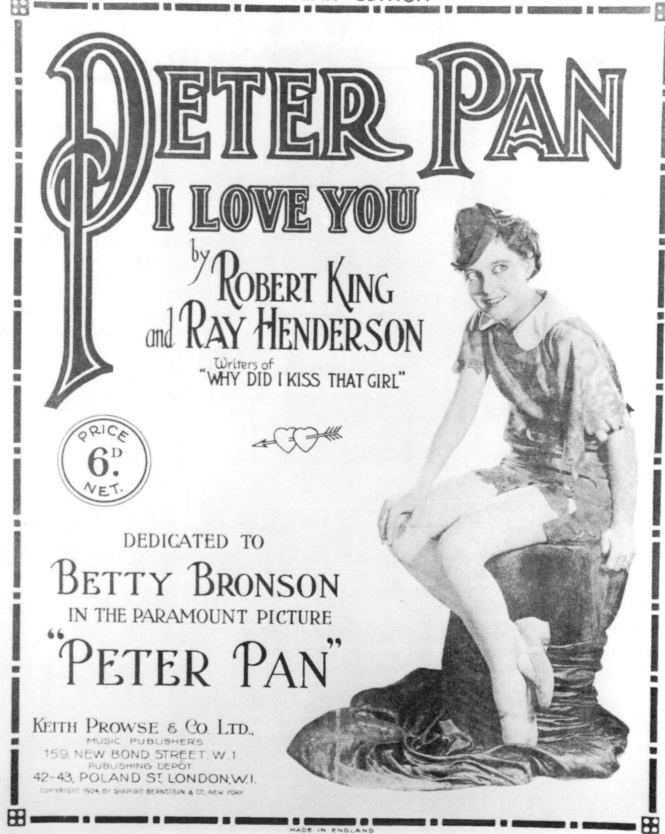

Peter Pan (1924), value $6.

A legendary song exploiting Valentino's death, value $20.

Our Dancing Daughters (1928), value $5.

Rudolph Valentino is a good subject for collectors of sheet music. Among the music on which he is featured is "Rudolph Valentino Blues" (1922), "You Gave Me Your Heart So I Gave You Mine" (1922) and, published in connection with *Blood and Sand*, "I'm Getting So Now I Don't Care" (1923), plus "That Night in Araby" (1926), published to promote *The Son of the Sheik*. Two songs were published as posthumous tributes to Valentino: "We Will Meet at the End of the Trail" (1926), written by Valentino's wife, Jean Acker, and "There's a New Star in Heaven Tonight" (1926), written by Jimmy McHugh and Irving Mills.

More unusual is the music composed to promote the film industry itself. As early as 1909, there was a song titled "The Vitagraph Girl," sung in theatres using song slides* to provide audiences with the words and offering plaudits to the leading lady of the Vitagraph Company, Florence Turner. Among the songs about the motion picture in general are "She's Only a Moving Picture" by C.E. Dittmann (1912); "Movie Rag" by J.S. Zamecnik (1912); "Oh! Oh! The Picture Show!" composer unknown (1913); "At the 10 Cent Movie Show" by Leo J. Curley and George Christie (1913); "Since Mother Goes to Movie Shows" by Chas. McCarron and Albert Von Tilzer (1916); "Since Sarah Saw Theda Bara" by Alex Gerber and Harry Jentes (1916); "Take Your Girlie to the Movies (If You Can't Make Love at Home)" by Edgar Leslie, Bert Kalmar, and Pete Wending (1919), and "At the Moving Picture Ball" by Joseph H. Santley (1920).

Unfortunately, specialist film bookshops tend to charge outrageous prices for film-related sheet music. I have seen the theme song from D. W. Griffith's *Hearts of the World* offered for as much as $50, although its value is certainly no more than $15. In purchasing sheet music it is well to bear in mind that no piece is worth more than $20, and that most film-related music can be purchased for under $10 if the collector confines his purchases to recognized dealers in sheet music.

Shirley A. Beavers (6191 Alkire Road, Galloway, Ohio 43119/614-878-5580) sends out quarterly lists, available at $2 each, of sheet music broken down by personalities and by subject matter, such as airplanes, circus, flowers, music boxes, and movies. She also lists the cover artists where identified. The bimonthly lists from Beverly A. Hamer (P.O. Box 75, East Derry, N.H. 03041/603-432-3528) are meticulous in detail. Most items are priced, but some are up for auction, and Ms. Hamer's lists are broken down by subjects such as patriotic, Prohibition and Temperance, and movie. There is absolutely no order to the voluminous listings from Lillian and Dulcina

1915 sheet music promoting the Mary Pickford vehicle, *Tess of the Storm Country,* value $10.

McNeill (1117 South Taylor Avenue, Oak Park, Ill. 60304/312-386-3318), but the McNeill sisters' lists are worth reading in detail if for no other reason than the highly personal comments that they make about the music and the stars associated with it. John C. Van Doren (35 Hart Avenue, Hopewell, N.J. 08525/609-466-2196) charges $1 for his lists, which arrange the sheet music by personality and by show and film titles.

All collectors of sheet music, film or non-film, are urged to join the National Sheet Music Society, "a non-profit educational organization whose membership seeks to save from oblivion the published sheet music of the American people. This music is rapidly disappearing in an 'instant stardom' age, where today's hit often becomes yesterday's forgotten song. The credo of this society is The Story of a Nation Is Told in Its Songs." Membership in the society entitles an individual to be listed in its directory, to receive a newsletter published ten times per year, and to attend regional meetings. For more information, readers are urged to contact Marilyn Brees, secretary of the National Sheet Music Society, at 1597 Fair Park Avenue, Los Angeles, Calif. 90041.

---

*For an overview of song slides, see "Romance and Joy, Tears and Heartache, and All for a Nickel" by John W. Ripley in *Smithsonian* magazine (March, 1982), pages 77-82.

7 Programs, Press and Campaign Books

In his 1915 volume, *Motion Picture Theatre Advertising* (current value $35), Epes Winthrop Sargent wrote, "No form of picture theatre advertising is so valuable to a house as a well printed and smartly edited program." Sargent's philosophy was one that held good through the late Twenties. Theatres produced not only their own programs, promoting anything from the current film to a month's films at one time, but also purchased beautifully printed, full-color souvenir programs that sold for 25 cents each and were generally published by Al Greenstone of New York.

Certainly programs for public consumption date back to at least 1910, if not earlier. Clune's Auditorium, which opened in Los Angeles on November 10, 1911, was typical of the major film houses that published their own weekly programs, providing cast lists and credits for the current presentations. When D.W. Griffith's *The Birth of a Nation* opened as *The Clansman* at Clune's Auditorium on February 8, 1915, the theatre provided its patrons with a twenty-page program or libretto containing a synopsis of the film and portraits with capsule biographies of the leading players. By the time *The Birth of a Nation* opened in New York, an elegant souvenir program was available to the audience. The original "libretto" from Clune's Auditorium is exceedingly rare and worth $75 or more, while the souvenir program currently sells for between $50 and $150.

Souvenir programs for many silent and talkie features can readily be found at between $10 and $25 apiece. Each program has a full-color illustrated cover, includes cast and technical credits, a plot synopsis, and articles on the production and the personalities involved. Among the programs recently seen for sale from Cinemabilia, Hampton Books, and Larry Edmunds

Bookshop were ones for *America* (1924), *Beau Geste* (1926), *The Big Parade* (1925), *The Broadway Melody* (1929), *The Covered Wagon* (1923), *Don Juan* (1926), *Hollywood Revue of 1929* (1929), *The Iron Horse* (1924), *The Jazz Singer* (1927), *King of Kings* (1927), and *The Son of the Sheik* (1926). Reproductions of a group of souvenir programs in their entirety may be found in a 1977 Dover publication, *Souvenir Programs of Twelve Classic Movies 1927-1941*.

In addition to such regular souvenir programs, collectors should be aware of the sumptuous programs printed for Hollywood premieres and for the opening of individual theatres. A one hundred page program, consisting mainly of advertisements, was produced for the opening of Grauman's Chinese Theatre in Hollywood on May 18, 1927, and the world premiere of Cecil B. DeMille's *King of Kings*. Another unusual program was that for the world's first twin premiere, Mary Pickford's *Sparrows* and Douglas Fairbanks' *The Black Pirate*, at Grauman's Egyptian Theatre in Hollywood on May 14, 1926. Nor should one ignore the leather-bound program for the world premiere of Howard Hughes' *Hells' Angels* on May 27, 1930, currently valued at $100.

In contradiction to Epes Winthrop Sargent's words, Frank H. Ricketson, Jr. wrote in *The Management of Motion Picture Theatres* (1938), "The old-style theatre program, issued for the convenience of the patrons, is passé, unless for a world's premiere, grand opening, anniversary, or some such event, which is enhanced by the publication of a souvenir of the occasion." Ricketson's comments seem to be basically accurate, for most theatres did cease to print their own programs by the late Thirties. One notable exception was Radio City Music Hall, which has always provided complimentary pro-

Souvenir program for *Star Wars* (1977), value $6.

grams for its patrons. Original Radio City Music Hall programs, in mint condition, from the Thirties currently sell for $7 each, those from the Forties for $5, those from the Fifties for $3, and those from the Sixties for $1.50. Sadly, Radio City Music Hall no longer offers film presentations on a regular basis, but its programs should continue to increase in value. Collectors should certainly consider acquiring copies of the Radio City Music Hall program for Abel Gance's *Napoleon,* presented on October 15–18, 1981. They can be purchased for $1 or less and are surely destined to increase considerably in value through the years.

Other programs of interest to collectors include those published every six weeks or so by London's National Film Theatre and which provide a wealth of succinct information on individual films and also the occasional special programs published by New York's Museum of Modern Art in connection with some of its major series and tributes, such as those in honor of M-G-M, Paramount, and Universal. Back in 1967, New York's

Gallery of Modern Art produced souvenir programs in conjunction with its tributes to Arthur Freed, Albert Lewin, Groucho Marx, W.C. Fields, Nazimova, Rouben Mamoulian, and Joseph Pasternak, among others. These programs can still be found in film bookshops for as little as $2 each and should increase considerably in value. Also selling for around $2 and worthy of consideration for collectors are the souvenir programs for such major film festivals as New York (from 1963) and Filmex in Los Angeles (from 1971).

Of course, souvenir programs have not completely disappeared. They are still published, particularly in connection with special film presentations, and, as the *Los Angeles Times* noted, ''These colorful programs have become as much a fixture of the lavish three-hour production as the intermission, and each new season brings another array of souvenirs for theater patrons.'' The chief source for current souvenir programs is Program Publishing Company (1472 Broadway, Suite 915, New York, N.Y. 10036), which did those for *The Longest*

Souvenir program for *Wings* (1927), value $20.

Program for world premiere of *Broadway Melody* at Grauman's Chinese Theatre, February 1, 1929, value $20.

TERRIFIC AS ALL CREATION!

Souvenir program for *Cimarron* (1931), value $20.

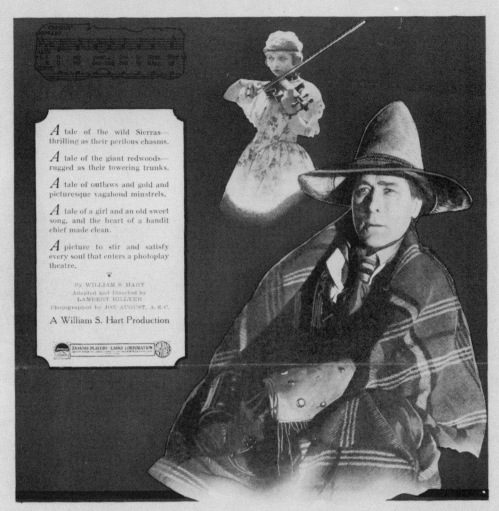

Exhibitor's press book for the 1920 William S. Hart vehicle, *The Testing Block,* value $50.

Program for world premiere of Joan Crawford's *Rain* at Grauman's Chinese Theatre, September 9, 1932, value $20.

An unusual souvenir program for the Grauman's Chinese Theatre presentation of *Queen Christina* (1933), with the cover in Swedish, value $25.

Darryl F. Zanuck's

WILSON

in TECHNICOLOR

Souvenir program for *Wilson (1944), value $10.*

Exhibitors' campaign book from the early Thirties for Mickey Mouse and Silly Symphony shorts, value $100.

Souvenir program for D.W. Griffith's *Way Down East* (1920), value $70.

PROGRAM

RKO-HILLSTREET THEATRE
FRIDAY EVENING, OCTOBER 21st

PART I

(a) 'SHAM POO, THE MAGICIAN'
with
Rosco Ates, Hugh Herbert, Dorothy Granger
An RKO-Headliner Comedy
Lou Brock, Associate Producer

(b) RKO-PATHE NEWS WEEKLY
Presents Latest World Events

(c) 'MICKEY'S NIGHTMARE'
A Walt Disney Cartoon Novelty

(d) MAX STEINER
and his RKO STUDIO ORCHESTRA
assisted by
SOL HOOPI'S HAWAIIAN CHORUS
Presenting a composition from 'The Bird of Paradise'

(Services of all of whom are donated
to the
MOTION PICTURE RELIEF FUND)

PART II

RADIO PICTURES, Inc.
DAVID O. SELZNICK, Executive Producer
Presents

JOHN BARRYMORE

in

'A Bill of Divorcement'
Directed by GEORGE CUKOR

Adaptation by	HOWARD ESTABROOK
Screen play by	HARRY WAGSTAFF GRIBBLE
From the play by	CLEMENCE DANE
Sound recorded by	GEORGE ELLIS
Photographed by	SID HICKOX
Assistant Director	DEWEY STARKEY
Technical Director	MARION BALDERSTONE

Hilary	JOHN BARRYMORE
Margaret	BILLIE BURKE
Sydney	KATHARINE HEPBURN
Kit	DAVID MANNERS
Dr. Alliot	HENRY STEPHENSON
Ray Meredith	PAUL CAVANAUGH
Aunt Hester	ELIZABETH PATTERSON
Bassett	GAYLE EVERS

This program presented under the auspices of
The MOTION PICTURE RELIEF FUND

Souvenir program for Katharine Hepburn's first feature, *A Bill of Divorcement* (1932), value $15.

Day, *Mary Poppins*, *West Side Story*, *Hawaii*, *The Happiest Millionaire*, *Cleopatra*, *Becket*, *The Fall of the Roman Empire*, *A Hard Day's Night*, *Star!*, *Chitty Chitty Bang Bang*, *Dr. Doolittle*, *Ben-Hur*, and many others. There is little question that the most sought-after current souvenir program is the original 1977 one for *Star Wars*, now selling at $5 a copy.

Besides film programs, some collectors are interested in theatre programs and playbills featuring film personalities in major plays. The best sources for these programs are Richard Stoddard (90 East Tenth Street, New York, N.Y. 10003/212-982-9440) and Front Row Center Theatre Memorabilia (8127 West Third Street, Los Angeles, Calif. 90048/213-852-0149).

"Press book" and "campaign book" are sometimes interchangeable. Press book should really refer to a studio-produced pamphlet intended exclusively for the press rather than for use by exhibitors in exploiting a film, but many exhibitor-oriented pamphlets are described as press books. Press books, campaign books—whatever one wishes to call them—date back to the early movie days. Film companies would put out single sheets, often as large as a page from a newspaper, with credit information and promotional stories on a movie. These sheets doubled as informational handouts for both newspapers and exhibitors, although some companies did produce material exclusively for the film journalist. For example, during World War I, the Selig Polyscope Company published a sheet titled *Paste-Pot and Shears* specifically for newspaper use.

The press book has now been superseded to a large extent by the press kit, a folder containing cast and technical credits, production information, a synopsis, biographical information on the players, director, and producer, along with a set of still photographs from the production. Press kits from current films vary in price according to whether the still photographs are intact and, of course, according to the popularity of the film. Certainly complete press kits on recent productions should sell for no more than $20. Without the stills they are worth little more than $2.

Campaign books used to be printed in a uniform size of 11 by 17 inches, but today are usually produced in an 8½ by 14 format. The books contain information on the film together with an illustrated listing of the type of publicity material available—everything from posters and lobby cards to bumper stickers and banners. It should be noted that not all campaign books are similar in size—the one for the Olsen and Johnson feature, *Hellzappopin* (1941), came in the form of a giant firecracker, 11½ by 22 inches.

Campaign books and press books can usually be found in the listings of most poster dealers (see Chapter 8) at

Tivoli Theatre, London, program for *I Was a Spy* (1933), starring Madeleine Carroll, value $10.

prices ranging from $10 to $100. A current listing from Stephen Sally (P.O. Box 646, New York, N.Y. 10036/212-246-4972) offers an interesting comparison in prices. Paramount press books for such features as *The Gracie Allen Murder Case* (1939), *Road to Singapore* (1940), and *Star Spangled Rhythm* (1942) sell for $10 each; those from Abbott and Costello Universal features of the Fifties for $25; those for Marilyn Monroe vehicles such as *How To Marry a Millionaire* (1953) and *The Seven Year Itch* (1955) for $50, and those for the science fiction classic, *The Day the Earth Stood Still* (1951) and the Katharine Hepburn vehicle, *Mary of Scotland* (1936), for $100.

Finally, as an adjunct to their campaign books, many of the studios produced lavish hard-cover promotional books for their upcoming films. These full-color volumes were published from the Twenties through the Forties, often promoting films that were never produced and announcing stars in features that subsequently starred another performer. Important historical documents as well as valuable collector's items, these books are good buys at $100 or $150, each.

8 Posters and Lobby Cards

Nothing in the film field has proven quite as collectible as posters and lobby cards, not only among film buffs but among a general public anxious to find any form of cheap and safe art investment. Graphic art has become a major collectible art form, and nowhere is this more apparent than in the area of film posters and lobby cards. As *Cosmopolitan* noted in 1976, "*All* posters are astute investments—last year's $15 purchase now costs $40."

Film posters follow in the tradition of the theatrical poster. The earliest known film-related posters are French, date from 1895, and promote the initial film screenings of the Lumiere brothers. They, along with Thomas Edison, are generally considered to be the creators of the motion picture. Posters promoting individual films did not come into general use in the United States until 1909, when exhibitors began demanding illustrative material to promote their movies. At first exhibitors asked for large photographic blowups for lobby display, but distributors and producers maintained that these were too expensive and suggested posters, lithographed in multiple colors. The exhibitors countered that posters looked sleazy and gave their theatres a bad reputation, but the distributors and producers insisted that posters were the cheapest and most advantageous method of promoting their new film releases.

One of the first companies to utilize film posters in a major way was the Kalem Company, which, in December of 1909, advertised to exhibitors that it was now able to provide a four-color product available directly from the A.B.C. Company of Cleveland, Ohio. Posters were a uniform 27 by 41 inches, a size already standardized in theatrical posters.

Various lithograph companies, notably Walter Color, Acme, J.H. Tooker, and H.C. Miner in New York, and Morgan, Otis, and A.B.C. in Cleveland, produced the posters, which did not even mention the names of the players at the beginning. (A few years back, a Mary Pickford collector was able to purchase a poster for a 1911 short titled *At the Duke's Command* for a very reasonable price, simply because the dealer was not aware that the actress depicted in the poster was an artist's likeness of America's sweetheart-to-be.)

Few of the artists responsible for film posters from the early days to the present signed their work. In the silent era, only one major figure emerged—Henry Clive, who was responsible for the poster characterizations of top Paramount stars such as Mary Pickford and Gloria Swanson. A former vaudevillian, Clive also worked as an illustrator for the Hearst newspaper syndicate, and his drawings graced many articles in *The American Weekly*. In later years, John Held, Jr. provided sketches for the poster of *Tin Hats* (1926), Thomas Hart Benton was hired to design the posters for 20th Century Fox's *The Grapes of Wrath* (1940), and Norman Rockwell was responsible for the posters of Orson Welles' *The Magnificent Ambersons* (1942), among others.

Lobby cards—as their name suggests—were produced for display in theatre lobbies and came into being in 1913. The earliest known lobby cards were produced by Universal in sets of four. Unlike later cards, some of these early ones were intended for vertical as well as horizontal display. The first cards were in shades of black and white or brown and white, and it was not until around 1917 that full-color ones began to appear. By the early Twenties all lobby cards were full color, with the exception of those for shorts and serials. All lobby cards are a standard size of 11 by 14 inches. There is no documentation as to why this size was adopted, but it is worth noting that eight lobby cards take up as much space as a folded one-sheet poster, and they always came in sets of eight, perhaps to aid in their packaging with a poster.

The sets of eight consisted of seven scene cards and one title card, but there were exceptions. Between 1919 and 1921, the Goldwyn Company produced nine lobby cards to a set, and in the Twenties Universal released sets of sixteen for such major productions as *The Hunchback of Notre Dame* (1923), *The Phantom of the Opera* (1925), *The Cat and the Canary* (1927), and *Showboat* (1929). In addition to regular lobby cards, during World War I some companies offered 8 by 10 still photographs in the form of lobby cards, complete with a title card and the advertising matter below each scene in the same manner as the captions appear on lobby cards. Also, at some point in the Thirties, the studios began to issue sets of four cards only for their shorts and serials releases.

In addition to posters and lobby cards, exhibitors were also offered 22 by 28 half-sheets, 14 by 36 inserts, and 14 by 22 window cards, all similar in size to advertising matter from the legitimate stage. These supplemental types of advertising cards and semi-posters date back to the early Twenties.

Through the Thirties all the studios produced their own posters and lobby cards, first printed by stone lithography, which gave a more vibrant color and better color texture to the posters. But beginning in the early Thirties the companies began to switch over to the less expensive, mechanized offset lithographic process. In 1940, National Screen Service, which had been in existence since 1919, took over the distribution of paper advertising materials for Paramount and RKO, and gradually all the studios turned over the production and distribution of such materials to N.S.S. Presently National Screen Service maintains ten branch offices throughout the United States, plus a home office in New York, a printing facility in Cleveland, and a complete film studio for the production of coming attraction trailers in London. In addition, N.S.S. operates Advertising Industries, which creates and manufactures frames and display cases, and Continental Lithograph, one of this country's largest lithographic printers of posters, etc. N.S.S. still services fifteen thousand theatres with trailers, posters, displays, and the like from the major distributors, although it should be noted that smaller companies such as New World and A.F.D. do not use the facilities of N.S.S.

National Screen Service is licensed to provide materials to theatres and to those associated with a specific film, but it does not provide anyone outside of

British dancer-singer-actress Jessie Matthews has always had a cult following in the United States. This poster from *Gangway* was sold two years ago by Eddie Brandt's Saturday Matinee for $150.

the industry with any of its products. Collectors will note that all posters and lobby cards contain a warning that such materials are the property of N.S.S. and must be returned after use. If it is any comfort, there has yet to be one case where N.S.S. has approached a dealer or collector and demanded such a return.

Collectors familiar with National Screen Service advertising matter will also be aware that the company provides a code number for each film on the lower left-hand corner. In addition, the letter "R" indicates that the advertising matter is for the reissue of the film, and the two figures following the "R" reveal the year of that reissue. Posters or lobby cards for reissues are, quite obviously, worth much less than advertising matter from the initial release. (Posters issued by the studio will have the leters "A," "B," "C," or "D" somewhere in the design to indicate which version they are.)

Lobby card for *Blood and Sand* (1922), value $175.

A crude lobby card, almost with a cutout effect, from the 1922 feature, *The Young Rajah*, value $250.

A lobby card from the 1929 Clara Bow feature, *The Saturday Night Kid*, value $75.

Poster for *The Phantom of the Opera* (1925), value $5,000.

One sheet posters are not the only size that have been printed. From the early days onwards, posters have been produced in three, six, twelve, and twenty-four sheet sizes. From a collector's point of view, these larger-size posters have little interest because of the space they would take to display. If you own a twenty-four sheet poster, you probably will not have a wall large enough for display (not to mention the amount of money you would need to pay for the framing of such a monstrosity), and the poster will have to remain permanently folded. Recent years have also seen the introduction of a new size of one-sheet poster, 30 by 40, usually issued in two versions and printed on a heavier stock paper that makes it impossible to roll the poster for storage or shipping.

The storage and preservation of posters is a very complex matter. Basically, posters should be stored flat in a dust-free atmosphere. The linen backing of posters is not always helpful to preservation because the glue used to affix the backing may have a detrimental effect on the poster itself. Because all posters have an acidic content and are gradually eating themselves away, the only ideal preservation would be a bath to remove the acid. Unfortunately such baths are usually only available at some museum locations and use is limited to the museum's own collection. One method to prevent the acid in a poster from affecting one laid on top or beneath it is to place sheets of acid-free paper between posters. Acid-free paper, along with museum-quality storage boxes for photographs, mounting boards, and framing accessories are available from the Light Impressions Corporation (439 Monroe Avenue, P.O. Box 940, Rochester, N.Y. 14603/800-828-6216). If a collector owns a poster of extreme value, the best course of action is to contact a conservation expert at a local art gallery or museum and seek guidance. Most commercial framing establishments are not equipped or qualified to provide professional advice on poster preservation or restoration.

In collecting lobby cards two fundamental rules apply: A complete set is always desirable and title cards—the first in each set announcing the title of the film and its stars—are always worth more than the remaining seven that depict scenes from the production. As a general rule, Larry Edmunds Bookshop always prices its title cards 25 percent higher than the other cards in the set.

The value of lobby cards, like any type of movie memorabilia, is governed by the celebrity or film they depict. The highest price ever paid for a single lobby card is believed to be $3,000 for a title card from *Dracula* (1931). As a general rule, lobby cards depicting principal characters in any of the following films now sell for $1,000 each: *King Kong* (1933), *Gone with the Wind* (1939), *The Wizard of Oz* (1939), *The Maltese Falcon* (1941), and *Casablanca* (1942). A lobby card from *Casablanca* that showed Ingrid Bergman, but not

Humphrey Bogart, was recently sold for $750.

Lobby cards from the silent era vary tremendously in price. Many from 1913–1919 of forgotten films or with forgotten stars, can be purchased for as low as $10 or $15. A lobby card from a Charley Chase comedy of the Twenties is now valued at $35, while one from a Buster Keaton feature from the same period is worth $175. Lobby cards depicting female silent stars are priced according to the current popularity of the actress: Blanche Sweet sells for $25, Leatrice Joy for $30, Betty Blythe for $35, and Viola Dana for $40. Viola Dana cards seem to have increased in value because she gained new fans when she appeared on the Thames Televison *Hollywood* series and she is still around and willing to autograph material.

A lobby card from an Alfred Hitchcock feature of the Forties currently sells for $40, while one from a Fifties Hitchcock feature can be purchased for $25 or $30. There are, of course, exceptions. Lesser known Hitchcock dramas, such as *I Confess* (1953) or *The Trouble with Harry* (1955) have lobby cards of little value when compared to one from a popular Hitchcock title such as *North by Northwest* (1959) or *Psycho* (1960). Lobby cards from early Chaplin shorts and features are very overpriced, but it is still possible to purchase one from *The Chaplin Revue* (1959) for as little as $25. Similarly, while lobby cards from the major horror films are valued in the hundreds of dollars, one from the Japanese horror feature, *Mothra* (1962), can cost as little as $10.

Ronald Reagan lobby cards continue to appeal to collectors. At a recent auction in Los Angeles, a set from *Tropic Zone* (1953) sold for $175, and another from *Hellcats of the Navy* (1957), the only film Reagan made with his wife, Nancy Davis, sold for $325.

From a purely aesthetic point of view, posters are far more attractive investments than lobby cards. The only negative aspect is that they take up more space and require more attention to store. The chief problem is that few vintage posters come on the market at reasonable prices because there is absolutely no one in America who is unaware of the value of such items. A few years ago it might have been possible to purchase a collection of one-sheet posters from the silent era for $10 or $15 per poster, but today there is little chance of buying anything from that period for under $100. Prices rise because dealers follow other dealers in their pricing. When Larry Edmunds sells a poster for $250, Eddie Brandt's Saturday Matinee will automatically raise its price on that same item accordingly. Eight years ago Larry Edmunds Bookstore placed an original poster for *Frankenstein* (1931) in its window priced at $1,000. It was sold within a week, and was last valued at $5,000.

In an article published in *The Connoisseur* (October,

1981), Charles Lockwood noted, "Although most pre-Second World War posters are attractive to look at and desirable to collectors, only a handful can be called artistically and historically significant. Most dealers and collectors agree that these few hundred posters share three qualities: good design and careful printing, an important film, and the star or stars depicted in a scene which captures the spirit of the movie. Significant American posters, to name a few, include *The Adventures of Robin Hood* (1938), *Casablanca* (1942), *Citizen Kane* (1941), *Gone with the Wind* (1939), *The Kid* (1921), *King Kong* (1933), *The Maltese Falcon* (1941), *The Phantom of the Opera* (1925), *The Thief of Bagdad* (1924), and *The Wizard of Oz* (1939)."

Posters from any of those films would sell today for $1,000 or more, but it is still possible to find some that, although perhaps not in the top echelon of poster or film art, are still attractive enough for display and important enough for investment purposes. An average M-G-M Lon Chaney poster would cost a minimum of $1,000 and posters from Chaney's Universal features, *The Phantom of the Opera* (1925) and *The Hunchback of Notre Dame* (1923), would sell for several thousand dollars. But a poster from a minor, early Chaney feature such as *The Shock* (1923) can still be purchased for around $500.

Posters for minor Bela Lugosi and Fred Astaire films still sell for under $50, while those from Spencer Tracy-Katharine Hepburn features remain bargains at under $200. In the area of science fiction and horror films, astronomical prices have been asked for posters from *M* (1931) and *The Cabinet of Dr. Caligari* (1919). An original German poster from Fritz Lang's 1926 futuristic drama, *Metropolis*, is said to be worth between $10,000 and $20,000—only four copies are known to exist. Yet it is still possible to purchase posters of Michael Landon in *I Was a Teenage Werewolf* (1957) for $100 or from *One Million Years B.C.* (1940) for less than $200. With the passing of time, posters from horror films of the Forties and Fifties cannot help but increase in value. Posters from the James Bond and Superman series are also well worth investigating as potential investments.

At present, some of the top personalities in posters include, in addition to Chaney (a poster of him in *The Unknown* (1927) sold three years ago for $2,000), Rudolph Valentino and Clara Bow, neither of whose posters are worth less than $500. Jeanette MacDonald-Nelson Eddy posters are valued at between $150 and $350 each, and Jean Harlow posters are now worth a minimum of $500. An original British poster from such an Alfred Hitchcock feature of the Thirties as *The 39 Steps* (1935) could now sell for $750. Humphrey Bogart posters vary tremendously in value. Better titles sell for $500 or more, while it is still possible to find one-sheet posters from Bogart "B" pictures for as little as $50 each.

Walter Plunkett with a gown he designed for Vivien Leigh to wear in *Gone with the Wind* (1939). In the unlikely event the costume ever came on the market it would sell for $12,000.

With so many of them around and easily accessible, Western stars continue to hold an interest for collectors of posters and lobby cards. John Wayne, Gene Autry, and Roy Rogers remain high in popular appeal—just as they were the screen's top Western personalities thirty and forty years ago. Their posters range in price from $50 to $175 and their lobby cards from $35 to $75. Among the minor Westerners, Jock Mahoney, Sunset Carson, Eddie Dean, Pat Buttram, Iron Eyes Cody, Yakima Canutt, and Penny Edwards continue to ride high both in the saddle and in popularity. Surprisingly, the truly great Western heroes of an earlier age, William S. Hart and Tom Mix, lack the appeal of these "B" Westerners of the Forties and Fifties.

One of the leading entrepreneurs in the Western field is Snuff Garrett, whose company, Nostalgia Merchant (6255 Sunset Boulevard, Suite 1019, Hollywood, Calif. 90028/213-464-1406), offers a wide range of videotapes of Republic Westerns as well as major features from that studio and RKO. In addition, Nostalgia Merchant has marketed a selection of limited edition, 24 by 30 posters featuring long-standing screen personalities, and autographed personally by each. Currently available, at between $100 and $125, are posters of Burt Reynolds (in

A selection of 20th Century-Fox posters featuring Betty Grable, value $50 each.

Lobby card for *The Kid Brother* **(1927), value $75.**

a limited edition of 2,000 prints), Shirley Temple (in a limited edition of 1,600), The Stars of Metro-Goldwyn-Mayer (in a limited edition of 2,000), Mae West (in a limited edition of 2,000), Johnny Weissmuller as Tarzan (in a limited edition of 1,500), Buster Crabbe as Flash Gordon (in a limited edition of 1,500), Clayton Moore and Jay Silverheels as the Lone Ranger and Tonto (in a limited edition of 1,500), Ray Bolger and Jack Haley in *The Wizard of Oz* (in a limited edition of 2,000), and The Stars of Republic Pictures (in a limited edition of 1,200). Each of these posters is as guaranteed a collector's item as it is possible to be—particularly now that a number of the featured stars are either dead or incapacitated—and should prove to be good investments.

Collectors interested in the poster painter's art should also be aware of a poster designed by Robert Peak and used as the cover illustration for the reprint of the 1937 edition of the *Academy Players Directory Bulletin*. Peak was also responsible for the posters for *West Side Story*, *Islands in the Stream*, *Rollerball*, *Star Trek: The Motion Picture*, *Superman*, *Pennies from Heaven*, and *Apocalypse Now*. Copies of Peak's poster, which features likenesses of the Thirties stars are available at $25 each from the Academy of Motion Picture Arts and Sciences (8949 Wilshire Boulevard, Beverly Hills, Calif. 90211).

It would be impossible to list all of the poster and lobby card dealers across the United States, many of whom operate almost on a hobby basis, appearing at one convention and then disappearing from view until the next. As posters became rarer, memorabilia dealers tend to have fewer and fewer from the Twenties and Thirties. The majority of such posters seem to be in private hands, and when they do come on the market it is usually for sale on consignment with a dealer or at an auction.

In Los Angeles, the following poster and lobby cards outlets along Hollywood Boulevard should be noted: Collectors Book Store, also known as Bennett's (6783 Hollywood Boulevard, Hollywood, Calif. 90028/213-467-3296); Larry Edmunds Bookshop (6658 Hollywood Boulevard, Hollywood, Calif. 90028/213-463-3273); and Hollywood Book and Poster Company (1706 North Las Palmas, Hollywood, Calif. 90028/213-465-8764). Eddie Brandt's Saturday Matinee (6310 Colfax Avenue/P.O. Box 3232, North Hollywood, Calif. 91609/213-506-4242) is as valuable a source for posters and lobby cards as for stills. Bob Colman's Hollywood Poster Exchange (965 North La Cienega Boulevard, Los Angeles, Calif. 90069/213-657-2461) offers many rare items. For those with an unlimited budget and a yen to acquire a poster or lobby card already framed, there is always Bijou (10250 Santa Monica Boulevard, Century City Shopping Center, Los Angeles, Calif. 90067/213-277-0637).

In New York, the mail order business of Sigmund Goode, The Movies (P.O. Box 639, New York, N.Y. 10011/212-929-6077), offers posters along with stills, scripts, and other memorabilia. Jerry Ohlinger's Movie Material Store (120 West Third Street, New York, N.Y. 10012/212-674-8474) has a wide variety of posters and black-and-white and color stills available to personal callers and by mail order. Ohlinger's current catalog includes a good sampling of posters from the Sixties onwards. He also carries a line of 21 by 29 reprints of classic posters at $3 each. Donald L. Velde (370 West Thirty-Fifth Street, New York, N.Y. 10001/212-563-2929) is an operation similar to National Screen Service and handles the publicity materials for independent and foreign film distributors such as New Yorker Films. However, unlike N.S.S., Donald L. Velde does sell to individuals at a standard fee of $2 per black-and-white still and $6 for each one-sheet poster.

Cine Monde (1488 Vallejo Street, San Francisco, Calif. 94109/415-776-9988) provides for $3 a massive, seventy-two page catalog of its poster holdings broken down by personality. Among the posters available at the time of writing were *To Have and Have Not* ($300), *Thunderball* ($110), *The Bride Came C.O.D.* ($150), *Daisy Kenyon* ($40), *Star Spangled Rhythm* ($35), *The Letter* (1940 version $400), *To Each His Own* ($20), *Hello Frisco* ($70), *Objective Burma* ($190), *Guess Who's Coming to Dinner?* ($12). *The Legend of Lylah Clare* ($10.50), *Kitty Foyle* ($65), and *The Longest Day* ($25). Cine Monde also sells lobby cards and other types of advertising material.

R. Neil Reynolds (Box 133, Waterford, Va. 22190/703-882-3574) is a mail order business specializing in all types of vintage posters, including film. A recent listing included a one-sheet poster of Glenn Tryon in *Dame Ahoy* (1930) for $75, a one-sheet of Betty Compson and Richard Dix in *The Stranger* (1924) for $95, and a one-sheet of Reginald Denny in *One Hysterical Night* (1929) for $85. A complete set of eight lobby cards of Theda Bara in *Salome* (1918) was priced at $350. A linen-backed poster from the 1941 version of Chaplin's *The Gold Rush* sold for $150, and an original three-sheet poster of the Marx Brothers in *Room Service* (1938) was $800. George Theofiles (Box 1776, New Freedom, Pa. 17349/717-235-4766) is another general dealer in antique posters, and his voluminous catalogs always offer a good selection of film subjects.

The Poster Emporium (5631 East 40 Highway, #24, Kansas City, Mo. 64128/816-921-5362) is another dealer with a huge catalog of posters and other advertising matter from 1944 to date, all very reasonably priced. The Movie Poster Place (P.O. Box 309, Lansdowne, Pa. 19050-0309/215-259-6592) publishes newspaper-size catalogs of posters, press books, stills, and even 35mm and 16mm trailers, with the bulk of the material dating from the Fifties onwards. The Movie Poster Place is

French poster for initial presentation of the Lumiere films in 1896, value $3,000.

presently offering 24 by 36 posters from *Friday the 13th Part 3* at $5 each, and every poster comes with a pair of 3-D glasses.

Cinema City (P.O. Box 1012, Muskegon, Mich. 49443/616-722-7760) specializes in recent posters, lobby cards, and stills from the Sixties onwards. Its catalogs are broken down by film title, with average prices for one-sheet posters being $20 for *Close Encounters of the Third Kind*, $35 for *Oklahoma*, $12.50 for *Raging Bull*, $40 for *Rocky Horror Picture Show*, $12.50 for *Poltergeist*, $40 for *The Exorcist*, and $11.50 for *Fort Apache: The Bronx*. The catalogs from Bill Luton (3568 Philsdale, Memphis, Tenn. 38111/901-743-7292 and 901-458-3702) are broken down by personalities as varied as Evelyn Ankers (a one-sheet from her 1943 vehicle, *All by Myself*, selling for $13), and Esther Williams (a one-sheet from her 1952 feature, *Million Dollar Mermaid*, selling for $12.50). Luton sells lobby cards and window cards as well as posters, and his holdings date back to the Twenties.

Other poster outlets include Duncan Poster Service (132½ North Beckley, Dallas, Tex. 75203/214-943-6918), and Memory Shop West (1755 Market Street, San Francisco, Calif. 94103/415-626-4873), which also offers lobby cards and stills from the silent era to the present. Last, but certainly not least, is the Texas Movie Emporium (P.O. Box 12965, Austin, Tex. 78711/512-458-2676). Proprietor Ed Neal is not only one of the stars of *The Texas Chain Saw Massacre* (Cinema City sells one-sheets at $75 each), but also the proud owner of one of the best selections of vintage one-sheet posters and lobby cards in the country.

9 Props,
Costumes and Novelty Items

The most famous movie prop ever to come up for sale must have been "Rosebud," the childhood sled of Charles Foster Kane in Orson Welles' classic drama *Citizen Kane* (1941). It was sold by the auction house of Sotheby Parke-Bernet in New York for $55,000 to director Steven Spielberg after it was put up for sale by a trio of owners. They acquired it from a studio guard who had retrieved it from a junk heap! However, no sooner was the sled sold than questions were raised as to its authenticity. Orson Welles pointed out the obvious when he noted, "I have a deep suspicion about that sled, because we burned it." Indeed, at the close of *Citizen Kane* one does see the Rosebud sled being consigned to the fire. The son of *Citizen Kane*'s screenwriter, Herman Mankiewicz, reported that his father had been given the sled used by the boy Kane in the film, and that the prop was still in his family. In addition, the Rosebud sled sold at auction was made of balsa wood and certainly could not have withstood the weight of even a child. It transpired that it was one of three prop sleds built for the film.

The Rosebud story reveals the major problem in acquiring famous, or even minor, props that were supposedly used in films. Studios do not keep records of which props were used in specific productions, and collectors must rely on their own intuition or, more probably, on still photographs that document the props in specific scenes. Interestingly, when Judy Garland's famous ruby slippers from *The Wizard of Oz* (1939) were auctioned off a few years ago for $15,000, similar questions to those regarding Rosebud were raised, and it was revealed that several pairs of ruby slippers were used in the movie. Even the feet of a star can get uncomfortable wearing one pair of shoes for hours on end. (It is an interesting and amusing fact that one of the gowns worn by Vivien Leigh in *Gone with the Wind* is authenticated in part by the perspiration stains still clearly visible under the armpits).

Props and costumes do not appear that frequently in the collector's market, and the sources for most of the material currently available were two famous studio auctions, one at M-G-M and another at 20th Century-Fox. The M-G-M auction began on May 3, 1970, and the items ran to five volumes of catalogs. Thirty-two auction sessions were held and more than 10,000 catalogs were sold at $10 each—and it is worth noting that today they are collector's items in their own right. Listed were antique furniture, vintage cars, weaponry, armor plate, wind machines, wagon wheels, and costumes such as the hobo hat worn by Fred Astaire in *Easter Parade*, Leslie Caron's peacock dress from *An American in Paris*, and Kim Novak's red crepe dress from *The Legend of Lylah Clare*.

Perhaps the auction did not generate the excitement hoped for by the studio and the auction house, but some items fetched fairly staggering prices. The Cotton Blossom riverboat built for *Showboat* sold for $15,000; the brass bed from *The Unsinkable Molly Brown* went for $3,000; Andy Hardy's 1931 Ford roadster raised $7,000; the witch's hat from *The Wizard of Oz* brought $450, and the wizard's suit from the same film was purchased for $650.

The 20th Century-Fox auction generated even less excitement. After all, M-G-M counted among its stars the likes of Judy Garland, Clark Gable, Lana Turner, Greta Garbo, and Jean Harlow, while the best Fox could come up with were Shirley Temple, Will Rogers, and Tyrone Power. In fact, there were two Fox auctions, both organized by Sotheby Parke-Bernet in 1971 and

1976. The first, and more important, ran from February 25 to 28 and from November 14 to 21, and included such items as Shirley Temple's toys from *Captain January* (sold for $1,065), a walnut chair that once held Humphrey Bogart ($350), a two-seat bicycle from *Hello, Dolly!* ($2,500), Tyrone Power's bed from *Blood and Sand* ($950), and the bicycle used in *Butch Cassidy and the Sundance Kid* ($3,100).

Studio auctions may be uncommon, but auctions of the possessions of Hollywood personalities happen quite frequently. One of the most famous was when the American Art Galleries of Beverly Hills in 1945 auctioned the Rudolph Valentino collection, removed from his former home, Falcon's Lair. The forty-eight page catalog of that auction is now a collector's item in its own right, selling for $100 a copy.

In more recent times—March 13 to 15, 1981—the J.M. Goodman Auction Gallery in Glendale auctioned more than two thousand items from the Mary Pickford estate. The auction was extraordinary because there appeared to be so much junk that had belonged to America's sweetheart, and because much of it sold for outrageously high prices. Charlene Tilton, the star of the CBS television series *Dallas*, was the highest bidder, buying almost $50,000 worth of items, including a vanity steamer trunk for $6,000 and a fourteen-karat gold vanity set monogrammed "MP" that fetched $3,750. Among the more interesting items auctioned were Pickford's costume from *Little Lord Fauntleroy* ($2,200), Rudolph Valentino's cape from *Blood and Sand* ($4,750), Pickford's parasol from *Rebecca of Sunnybrook Farm* ($700), Douglas Fairbanks' cape from *The Mark of Zorro* ($1,800), and Miss Pickford's curling iron ($200).

Bette Midler purchased some Pickford costumes, as well as an oil painting of the actress, but one of the major bidders here as well as at the M-G-M and 20th Century-Fox auctions was Debbie Reynolds, who owns what must surely be one of the finest private collections of Hollywood costumes and props. Other private collections of similar materials are those owned by Debbie Reynolds' associate, John LeBold, and by actress Jane Withers.

Interest in motion picture costumes was initially stimulated by the Metropolitan Museum of Art exhibit of 1975, "The Romantic and Glamorous Years of Hollywood Costume Design." It featured Edith Head's costumes for Ginger Rogers in *Lady in the Dark* and Mae West in *She Done Him Wrong*; Adrian's costumes for Joan Crawford in *The Bride Wore Red* and Greer Garson in *Pride and Prejudice*; Helen Rose's costume for Grace Kelly in *The Swan*; John Truscott's costume for Vanessa Redgrave in *Camelot*; and Sir Cecil Beaton's costume for Audrey Hepburn in *My Fair Lady*. However, some institutions had been quietly collecting costumes and

props long before then. One such establishment is, surprisingly, the Los Angeles County Museum of Natural History, which owns Mark Pickford's costume from *Dorothy Vernon of Haddon Hall*, Tom Mix's hat, Harold Lloyd's spectacles, Lon Chaney's makeup kit, W.C. Fields' pool cue, Buster Keaton's porkpie hat, and *King Kong*'s articulated hand.

I mention these collectors and institutions because props and costumes so seldom come on the market. There is a shop called The Movie Set (3266 Cahuenga Boulevard West, North Hollywood, Calif. 90068), which specializes in antique motion picture clothing, but that is about it. Collectors should also check the catalogs of the Berry Auction Company (8380 Santa Monica Boulevard, Los Angeles, Calif. 90069/213-650-1223), recent items from which have included a ten-gallon Stetson signed by six hundred Hollywood personalities (sold for $1,900), a receipt for cinnamon toast and two cups of coffee at a San Francisco hotel signed by John Lennon ($135), and Bela Lugosi's personal playscript for *Dracula* ($1,000).

The Berry Auction Company generally features a good selection of animation cels (acetate sheets the animators use to draw the individual pictures for a cartoon), and these cels appear to be a good investment. One reason is that, as Din Luboviski, co-owner of Larry Edmunds Bookshop, points out, animators are so obsessed with their craft they are some of the most avid collectors and continually push prices up. Original cels from Walt Disney's *Snow White and the Seven Dwarfs* are valued at $2,500, but it is still possible to pick up cels from recent animated television series for anything between $5 and $20. The Berry Auction Company recently sold a cel from a Pink Panther cartoon for only $22.50.

One of the first pieces of film-related music to be recorded was the love theme (by Joseph Carl Breil) from D.W. Griffith's *The Birth of a Nation* (1915). However, the music was recorded as "The Perfect Song," the theme song from the popular CBS radio series, *The Amos and Andy Show*. More recently, collectors have been taking a serious interest in the acquisition of film soundtracks on record and film-related LPs, and the majority—provided they were kept in mint condition—have risen in value many hundred percent. Two good reference volumes on the subject are *Hollywood on Record: The Film Stars' Discography* by Michael R. Pitts and Louis H. Harrison (Scarecrow Press, 1978), and *Show Music on Record* by Jack Raymond (Frederick Ungar, 1982). Also useful is *Movie/TV Soundtracks & Original Cast Albums Price Guide* by Jerry Osborne (published in 1981 by O'Sullivan, Woodside & Co., 2218 East Magnolia, Phoenix, Ariz. 85034).

Another area that boasts many avid collectors concerns paper dolls of favorite film personalities, novelties that

An early advertisement for Walt Disney's "Alice" cartoons clipped from a Twenties trade paper, value $6.

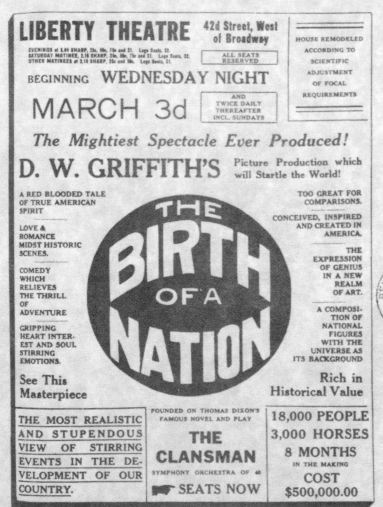

A collage of advertisements for *The Birth of a Nation* (1915), stamped with the first day of issue for the D.W. Griffith commemorative stamp (1975), value $10.

date back to the days when Mary Pickford and Charlie Chaplin were featured as paper dolls that were cut out and dressed in cut-out clothing. There are many books available dealing with the hobby, including *Shirley Temple Dolls and Collectibles* by Patricia R. Smith (published in 1979 by Collector Books, P.O. Box 3009, Paducah, Ky. 42001); *Paper Dolls of Famous Faces* by Jean Woodcock (published in 1980 by Hobby House Press, Cumberland, Md. 21502); *Doll Collectors' Treasures Volume 3 Featuring "Little Miss Shirley Temple"* by Laurel M. Dicicco (published in 1981 by the author at 14916 Cholame, Victorville, Calif. 92392); and *The Paper Doll* by Barbara Chaney Ferguson (published in 1982 by Wallace-Homestead Book Co., 1912 Grand Ave., Des Moines, Ia. 50305). Dover Publications has produced a series of paperback volumes on paper dolls featuring Vivien Leigh, Carmen Miranda, Marilyn Monroe, Rudolph Valentino, and John Wayne.

Other paper items of novelty interest include bookplates. Original bookplates designed for Joan Crawford sell for $10 each, while those designed by art director/production designer William Cameron Menzies for Rudolph Valentino are priced as high as $25. A bookplate of Mabel Normand or John Gilbert can inflate the value of a common book item more than 700 percent. Coming attraction advertising flyers given away by theatres as promotions are excellent collectibles for persons with limited space and limited funds. While a flyer advertising a Valentino or a Chaplin feature may be sold for as much as $10, the majority of them can be purchased for as little as $2 or $3.

Cigarette cards featuring film personalities, the British equivalent of baseball cards, have become increasingly popular with collectors. Each set of fifty cards usually comes with an album with space for each card and a capsule biography of the performers. In Britain, a set of cigarette cards without an album can be purchased for as little as $10, but in this country a complete set with an album from the John Player and Sons tobacco company currently sells for $100. There was at least one German set of two hundred cigarette cards produced by Zigarettenfabrik Monopol in the Thirties.

Surprisingly, material relating to the Academy Awards presentations currently have little interest and can be purchased fairly cheaply. But programs and posters, which are produced in very limited numbers, from past Oscar shows would seem to be good investments, and it is still possible to purchase copies of recent programs directly from the Academy of Motion Picture Arts and Sciences (8949 Wilshire Boulevard, Beverly Hills, Calif. 90211). No Oscar will ever legitimately turn up for sale, but it is possible to find a number of curiosities relating to the Awards, including matchbooks, postcards, invitations, and tickets to the shows. Just as popular as the Academy Awards are the

Life Achievement Awards of the American Film Institute, given since 1973, and which have honored the likes of John Ford, Bette Davis, James Cagney, Alfred Hitchcock, James Stewart, and John Huston. Programs from this presentation will also become collector's items, and it is possible, yet again, to purchase recent programs directly from the American Film Institute (Kennedy Center, Washington, D.C. 20566).

It is impossible to document the range of novelty items associated with the motion picture. The idea for promoting films and personalities through such material appears to have originated in about 1913, and, of course, it is even more of a big business today than it ever was. Some of the earliest novelty items included notepads with photographs of silent stars on their covers (they are still marketed today, except that it is Mickey Mouse or John Travolta who grace the covers rather than Beverly Bayne and Francis X. Bushman). Also dishes with portraits of stars such as Blanche Sweet and Gloria Swanson at their centers, dating from 1915 to 1919 and now valued at $25 and up; pin buttons of Carl Laemmle (the head of Universal Studios) with small banners attached announcing, "We Are on Our Way to Universal City"; and souvenirs from the original Universal Studio Tours, introduced in 1916. Currently valued at $100 is a complete set of playing cards from about 1915, with each card featuring a different star and Chaplin, of course, as the Joker.

A full-color advertisement for a 1935 Laurel and Hardy feature, *Bonnie Scotland*, taken from a contemporary trade paper, value $5.

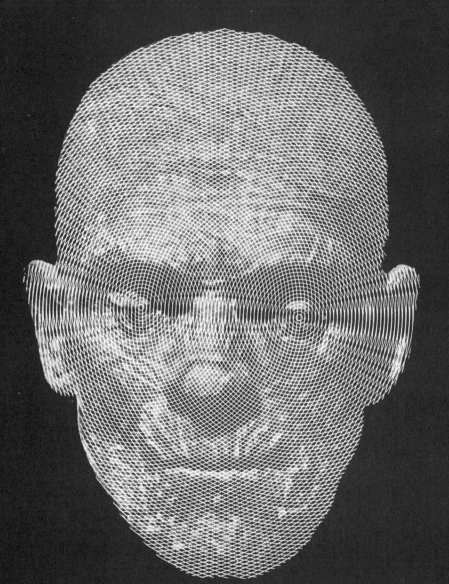

"It couldn't be done"— So Universal did it!

The Mummy
(A KARLOFF Classic)

Advertisement for the Boris Karloff horror film, *The Mummy*, clipped from a 1932 trade paper, value $5.

William S. Hart photograph given away with 1919 issue of *Picture Show*, value $5.

the rate of one per month. These spoons now sell for $12 or more each.

Tin boxes, originally manufactured to hold candy and featuring colorful likenesses of Wallace Reid, Rudolph Valentino, and others on their lids, were produced in the early Twenties and have been known to sell today for as much as $50 each. Cosmetic lines and toiletries would often feature film personalities. Peggy Hopkins Joyce had her own cosmetic line, as did Zsa Zsa Gabor in more recent years. In the early Thirties one could purchase popsicles that came with coins the size of a nickle that featured contemporary celebrities such as Marion Davies and Irene Dunne.

From the Thirties, novelty items include a Shirley Temple mug (given away by Gold Medal Foods in 1935), a Sonja Henie coloring book from 1939, and a 1941 Betty Grable paint book. In 1935, Ben Smiley children's clothes featured the Columbia cartoon characters "Scrappy" and "Margy." Particularly rare items are lead-cast models of mama, papa, and baby lion from the 1938 M-G-M Sales Conference. Buttons featuring pictures of film personalities were mass-produced in the hundreds of thousands in the Twenties, Thirties, and Forties, but are seldom seen today and sell for $5 and up. Buttons were just one of the many Tom Mix-related items. They also included comics, toy guns, rings, and even gloves, but the majority of these items related not to Tom Mix the film personality, but to the NBC radio series, *The Tom Mix Ralston Straightshooters*, which utilized the star's name but not the star. For further information on Western-related novelties, readers are referred to *Six Gun Heroes: A Price Guide to Movie Cowboy Collectibles* by Theodore L. Hake and Robert D. Cauler (Wallace-Homestead, 1976).

A novelty item that has particular appeal to those who grew up in the Thirties or Forties is a Dixie Cup lid. For five cents, children could purchase a cup of ice cream, and on the underside of the lid would be a photograph of a film personality such as Jean Harlow, Bette Davis, Gene Autry, or Buster Crabbe. Despite having been produced in the millions, Dixie Cup lids, because of their short life, have not survived and seem to be exceedingly rare.

The collecting of novelty items can be more fun and require more sleuthing than the acquisition of any other type of movie memorabilia. Flea markets and paper shows are the natural habitats of such items and their collectors. Additionally, in Los Angeles there are a number of shops specializing in this type of material, the best of which are Bijou (Century City Shopping Center, 10250 Santa Monica Boulevard, Los Angeles, Calif. 90067/213-277-0637); Chic a Boom (6905 Melrose Avenue, Hollywood, Calif. 90038/213-931-7441); Chuck and Rita's (5515 Lankershim Boulevard, North Holly-

About 1916, the Kahn-Beck Company of Los Angeles manufactured boxes of candy, marketed as Reel Chocolates, that had likenesses of Mabel Normand and J. Warren Kerrigan on their lids. The same company also distributed a Charlie Chaplin Nougat Bar, which might be more than a little stale today, but would still be a bargain for $20. Around 1920, the first series of silver-plated spoons with heads of movie personalities on the tips of the handles were sold in a set of seven or eight. In 1925, the Hearst newspaper chain released a set of twelve such spoons, giving them to new subscribers at

wood, Calif. 90068/213-761-2201); Nickelodeon (13820 Ventura Boulevard, Sherman Oaks, Calif. 91423/213-981-5325); and Scroungers (12041 Magnolia Boulevard, North Hollywood, Calif. 91607/213-762-0575).

Those collectors interested in science fiction and fantasy films and planning to visit Los Angeles should be sure to contact the Ackerman Archives (2495 Glendower Avenue, Hollywood, Calif. 90027/213-666-6326), which houses the personal collection of more than 200,000 items belonging to Forrest J. Ackerman, the man responsible for *Famous Monsters of Filmland*. The collection, which is open by appointment only, contains posters, books, and such esoteric items as props from the original *King Kong* and *The Creature from the Black Lagoon*.

Finally, for this type of material, together with everything else discussed here, there are two conventions that should not be missed. Both include screenings of rare films, personal appearances by film personalities of the past, and dealer rooms. The oldest is Cinecon, now in its nineteenth year after being organized by a group of film collectors who call themselves the Society for Cinephiles. The Cinecon is held each year in a different city—in 1982 it took place in Davenport, Iowa, and in 1983 in Chicago. Since it is organized on a voluntary basis, there is no permanent, central address for information. The easiest way to locate news on the Society for Cinephiles and the Cinecon is in the pages of *Classic Images* (P.O. Box 809, Muscatine, Ia. 52761).

The Movie/Video Expo of the National Film Society is now in its eighth year, and is always held at the Sheraton Universal Hotel in North Hollywood, California. The dealer room there is always much bigger than the one organized by Cinecon and is devoted almost exclusively to paper items rather than to films, which always comprise a good proportion of the materials being sold at Cinecon. At the 1982 Movie/Video Expo, more than fifty dealers were doing a thriving business. The National Film Society also publishes *American Classic Screen* for its members and is located at 8340 Mission Road, Suite 106, Shawnee Mission, Kan. 66206/913-341-1919.

Cinecon takes place over the Labor Day weekend, while Movie/Video Expo is held on the last weekend in October. Both provide unique opportunities for dealers and collectors to get together, examine new materials that have come on the market, and check current prices. These conventions help turn what can become a solitary hobby into an enthusiastic venture that can be shared with others. Happy collecting!

Edith Head with the suits she designed for Robert Redford and Paul Newman to wear in *The Sting* (1973).

Theda Bara's bookplate, value $25.

An assortment of Dixie Cup lids, value $5 each.

Since the Mary Pickford auction a considerable amount of Pickfordiana has become available to collectors, such as this note card showing Pickfair.

A painting by director Rex Ingram. In recent years, paintings by film personalities have been sought by collectors. Among those who presently paint as a hobby are silent stars Mary Brian, Janet Gaynor, and Alice Terry. Cult director James Whale was also a painter in his spare time, but seldom signed his paintings, which makes those with a signature almost double the worth of those without.

Bibliography

Axe, John. *The Collectible Dionne Quintuplets.* Cumberland, Md.: Hobby House Press, 1977.

——. *Collectible Sonja Henie.* Cumberland, Md.: Hobby House Press, 1979.

——. *The Encyclopedia of Celebrity Dolls.* Cumberland, Md.: Hobby House Press, 1983.

Camner, James, and Lanigan, Neale W. *Film Autographs 1894-1941.* W. Neale Lanigan, Jr. and La Scala Autographs, 1978.

Chaneles, Sol. *Collecting Movie Memorabilia.* New York, N.Y.: Arco, 1977.

Christensen, Roger and Karen. *The Ultimate Movie, TV and Rock Directory.* Cardiff-by-the-Sea, Calif.: Cardiff-by-the-Sea Publishing Company, 1982.

Dicicco, Laurel M. *Doll Collectors' Treasures Volume 3 Featuring "Little Miss Shirley Temple."* Laurel M. Dicicco, 1981.

Dietz, James S., Jr. *Price Guide and Introduction to Movie Posters and Movie Memorabilia.* James S. Dietz, Jr., 1982.

Ferguson, Barbara Chaney. *The Paper Doll.* Des Moines, Iowa: Wallace-Homestead Book Company, 1982.

Gilbert, George. *Collecting Photographica.* New York, N.Y.: Hawthorn Books, 1976.

Hake, Theodore, L., and Cauler, Robert D. *Six Gun Heroes: A Price Guide to Movie Cowboy Collectibles.* Des Moines, Iowa: Wallace-Homestead Book Company, 1976.

Hamilton, Charles. *Collecting Autographs and Manuscripts.* Norman, Okla.: University of Oklahoma Press, 1974.

Harmon, Jim. *Jim Harmon's Nostalgia Catalogue.* Los Angeles, Calif.: J.P. Tarcher, 1973.

Kobal, John, and Wilson, V. A. *Foyer Pleasure: The Golden Age of Cinema Lobby Cards.,* n.p.: Album Press, 1982.

Lahue, Kalton C. *Collecting Classic Films.* New York, N.Y.: Hastings House, 1970.

Limbacher, James L. *Feature Films on 8mm, 16mm, and Videotape.* New York, N.Y.: R.R. Bowker, 1982.

Maltin, Leonard, ed. *The Whole Film Sourcebook.* New York, N.Y.: New American Library, 1983.

Maltin, Leonard, and Greenfield, Allan. *The Complete Guide to Home Video.* New York, N.Y.: Harmony Books, 1981.

McKee, Gerald. *Film Collecting.* Scarsdale, N.Y.: A.S. Barnes, 1978.

Mebane, John. *Collecting Nostalgia.* New York, N.Y.: Arlington House, 1972.

The National Video Clearinghouse. *The Video Source Book.* Syosset, N.Y.: The National Video Clearinghouse, 1982.

Osborne, Jerry. *Movie/TV Soundtracks and Original Cast Albums Price Guide.* Phoenix, Ariz.: O'Sullivan, Woodside and Co., 1981.

Smith, Patricia R. *Shirley Temple Dolls and Collectibles.* Paducah, Ky.: Collector Books, 1979.

Weiss, Ken. *The Movie Collector's Catalog.* Alhambra, Calif.: Cunningham Publishing, 1977.

Westin, Helen. *Introducing the Song Sheet.* Nashville, Tenn.: Thomas Nelson, 1976.

Woodcock, Jean. *Paper Dolls of Famous Faces.* Cumberland, Md.: Hobby House Press, 1980.

Index

About the Author

Anthony Slide has been involved with the cinema professionally as a working film scholar for the past fifteen years. Born in 1944 in Birmingham, England, he served as assistant editor of the British annual *International Film Guide* from 1968 to 1971. During that same period, he also edited and published *The Silent Picture* and programmed various series at London's National Film Theatre—including Britain's first silent film festival.

In 1971 he came to the United States as a Louis B. Mayer Research Associate with the American Film Institute's Center for Advanced Film Studies in Los Angeles. He continued his association with the A.F.I. in Wash-

ington, D.C., where he set up the 1911–1920 volume of the *American Film Institute Catalog* and served as the institute's associate archivist. He was at one time responsible for the acquisition and preservation of more than 2,000 films in the National Film Collection at the Library of Congress.

In 1975, Mr. Slide returned to Los Angeles to become resident film historian of the Academy of Motion Picture Arts and Sciences, a post which he held until 1980. During those years he served as head of the National Film Information Service, organizing in-house exhibits and coordinating more than fifty film events.

Mr. Slide has presented film programs at the Library of Congress, the Museum of Modern Art, the Sinking Creek Film Celebration in Nashville, Tennessee, Filmex in Los Angeles, and at the Pacific Film Archives in Berkeley, California. He has produced and directed a thirty-minute documentary on silent screen star Blanche Sweet, served as consultant for the popular TV series *That's Hollywood*, and worked on documentaries for Ulster and German television.

Mr. Slide has written many articles on the history of the cinema and for five years contributed a monthly column to *Films in Review*. He also notes that he has made something of a habit of writing articles for the premiere issues of various magazines, including *American Film*, *Focus on Film*, and *The Quarterly Review of Studies*. He has written more than a dozen books on film history and has recently started to write on vaudeville, radio, and television. Mr. Slide is also editor of the *Filmmakers* series of books published by Scarecrow Press.